Playing with Fish and Other Lessons from the North

Playing with Fish

and Other Lessons from the North

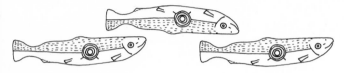

Robert J. Wolfe

The University of Arizona Press

Tucson

The University of Arizona Press

© 2006 Robert J. Wolfe

All rights reserved

∞ This book is printed on acid-free, archival-quality paper.

Manufactured in the United States of America

11   10   09   08   07   06   6   5   4   3   2   1

Library of Congress Cataloging-in-Publication Data

Wolfe, Robert James.

Playing with fish and other lessons from the North / Robert J. Wolfe.

p. cm.

Includes bibliographical references.

ISBN-13: 978-0-8165-2485-3 (pbk. : alk. paper)

ISBN-10: 0-8165-2485-8 (pbk. : alk. paper)

1. Human ecology—Alaska. 2. Human ecology—California. 3. Indigenous peoples—Ecology. 4. Human-animal relationships—Alaska. 5. Human-animal relationships—California. 6. Alaska—Environmental conditions. 7. California—Environmental conditions. I. Title.

GF504.A4W65 2006

304.209798–dc22

2005027955

This book is for Sylvia, who loves being warm.

Contents

Playing with Fish and Other Lessons from the North

1

Passing between Worlds

Lives Built on Rock and Sand

I was almost born in a bean field, passing between worlds. This may sound remarkable, but it's not. It was commonplace for the twentieth century. Likely you too were almost born in a bean field, or a place like to it, a locality, a time, or a people passing rapidly away into something else. My particular field was lima beans. I missed it by two years. The bean field sat sandwiched between humble beach dunes along the Pacific coastline and the sprawl of cities that, soon after my birth, seamlessly merged into the megalopolis of Los Angeles. California appears in the stories I tell my children because of this fortuitous birth. At midcentury, California was bursting at the seams, filling her cities to spillover, leapfrogging New York to become America's most populous place. California thrust herself high, the nation's bright icon for quick wealth, alternative lifestyles, and cutting-edge technologies. I became a child of that place and time, tarrying long enough so that half of my own children were born Californians. But the other half are Alaskans. At another extreme, Alaska appears in my life stories too. When I went there in my late twenties, I found a land empty of people and full of promise. Alaska, America's other icon of greatness, overshadowed even California, her last great frontier of rugged individualism, her remnant of nature writ large, still raw and untamed. Alaska became my other home, where I moved, worked twenty years, and departed, forever changed. In my life, I've passed between several worlds. But in this past century of mass human migrations for Earth's people, this too is nothing remarkable. Likely you have too. What matters is which worlds we choose to make home.

The bean fields rate a few sentences in California's history as told by Kevin Starr, the Golden State's librarian and prodigious historian. After the Second World War, veterans flooded back to America. The nation was poised for postwar booms in babies, economies, and profiteering. In California, industrialist Henry J. Kaiser, retooling from war industries, cast an eye to housing. According to Kevin Starr, Kaiser envisioned mass-produced single-family houses for returning veterans, well built, efficient, with respectable amenities, and above all, affordable, especially with no-down government loans. Owning a Kaiser-built house would renew a veteran's stake in society. In 1948 Kaiser's vision became reality with the completion of 5,492 new homes on what were formerly bean fields astride the Los Angeles municipal airport. Fifty-five hundred new stake holds driven into the ground. I was born into Kaiser's dream two years later, a postwar baby boomer.

Of course, before the lima bean fields became prefabricated suburbs, this place contained other worlds. Briefly, the area was a Spanish land grant with cattle grazing the coastal prairie. Before that it was a homeland for families of the Tongva-Gabrieleño tribes. Before that, it was a bluff overlooking a grasslands basin filled with mastodons, saber-toothed cats, dire wolves, and giant sloths, hunted by other peoples and tribes. The prehistoric bones of those ancient pasts still bubble up with the tar beneath the shining skyscrapers of the Miracle Mile. Some of these worlds lie hidden just beneath our feet. Others surround us still, just diminished and momentarily forgotten.

As a child, I played on the beach dunes beside my home. I remember sugary sand and brilliant green mats of ice plant bursting with red-apple blooms, falling to a flat Pacific. Slipping on dunes was a delight, a metaphor of childhood instructions. Build on rock, not sand. This I learned as a child, taught to me by family. We were Pacific Slope Brethren. That was my community. We were among those Brethren who had migrated west, away from the Anabaptist strongholds of rural Pennsylvania and Virginia's Shenandoah Valley, where the Brethren lived alongside other good neighbors—the Amish, Mennonites, and Friends—historic peace churches constructing peaceable kingdoms of heaven on earth. We were among the wayward Brethren oddly misplaced in the west. A fool builds a life on sand. I learned this, an enigmatic parable, wisdom I have come to trust. I teach the same to my children. Build lives on solid rock.

Yet the slippery dunes were ancient. Who knew? The ridge of dunes along Santa Monica Bay near my childhood home were so old, rare life had evolved in their shifting sands. I didn't know it was a world in itself. The ancient dunes gave foundation to complex communities of plants with names like coastal buck-wheat, deerweed, beach primrose, pigmy stonecrop, and California everlasting. A delicate butterfly, El Segundo Blue, wove its chrysalis above the sands, there and only there in all the earth. A lizard named *Aniela pulchra* wriggled like a snake through these dunes. It had done so for so long it had lost its legs. It's hard to comprehend sand that stable and enduring.

Throughout my youth, I watched Los Angeles push itself to the very edge of this ancient world, covering the small dunes with progress. Expensive beach homes arose on the hillocks overlooking the steely waters. Sewage plants and oil refineries spread out, perched on the bluffs, pumping effluent to and crude oil from the sea. The airport expanded continuously, extending its runways ever nearer the shore. As a teen, I walked the beach ridges beneath the deafening roar of jets, one passing up or coming down each minute or so, trafficking the new Californian lifestyles and cutting-edge technologies to worlds beyond the wide Pacific. I walked the disappearing dunes, unaware of the world of legless lizards and blue butterflies just beneath my sliding feet.

It's said that anthropology draws its stock from the marginalized, the men and women forced to society's fringes, peering from the edges of mainstreams and privileged classes, shut out by their Jewishness or gender or migrant status. The people who called themselves Brethren wore their peculiarity without com-plaint, their funny beards, their plain prayer veils. They communed in simple gatherings for foot washings and love feasts, resisted the social creep of consum-erism, military conscription, and other destructive trends, a people living *in* but not *of* the world. We were less visibly peculiar on the Pacific slope, scattered and acculturating and wondering what we were all about. Perhaps as a child of Pacific Slope Brethren, I was born to be marginal, born for anthropology. In any event, I became an anthropologist, but not in the classical tradition of Indi-ana Jones, tomb raiding for university museums. Nor was I a stones-and-bones paleoanthropologist uncovering prehistory in the quest for human origins. I fell in with the Margaret Mead crowd, studying human cultures for who knows what. At UCLA my specialty emerged — the hunting peoples of North America, especially the Far North. I began researching subsistence economies of Alaska Natives, completing the terminal degree in 1979 while teaching across town at USC, not knowing this was just a beginning.

The year before my personal milestone, forced by social turmoil and po-litical necessity, Alaska passed its first subsistence law. The law's intent was to protect the hunting peoples of the North. The federal government followed suit two years later. For the first time, laws recognized something called *subsistence*, customary and traditional ways of living, something indigenous, good, and threatened. But the new laws put government in a bind. What should be protected? And who? To implement them, the state needed guidance, a program for documenting subsistence in the villages of the Far North. By this time my personal life was in shambles. My first marriage was ending, my family dispersing, my vision clouded. In a life-changing move, I signed on. With about two dozen others, I found myself put within the state's Fish and Game Department, a cultural anthropologist peculiarly set among big-game biologists, commercial fish managers, and sport fish advocates. I came alone to Alaska, America's last frontier, divorced from my old life, distanced from the cultural centers of my youth, charged with documenting traditional ways of living. My personal education about other worlds would begin in earnest.

My first home was in Bethel, a small center of trade and government near the Bering Sea. This was not a mass-produced Kaiser-tract home. A feisty Irish carpenter had built it. When I rented it, the Irishman griped about shoddy work by a subcontracting plumber. He wasn't going to pay for slipshod work, he groused. He can take it to court, but he's not getting paid. I learned that for rent in Bethel I got local gossip along with a roof over my head.

The house sat on pilings above a pad of sand dumped on the tundra, like many others in town. I asked the Irishman, "Why do you build on stilts above sand pads?" "Because of this land," he said, sweeping his arm in a vast circle around him, a flat, treeless delta of water and partially frozen alluvium stretching toward a distant sea. The tundra swallows houses. The freeze-and-thaw lifts, tilts, and sucks them down. Heat from the house's belly turns the flat tundra to muck, accelerating its destruction. Pilings create empty space that buffers a house from the frozen ground. In this way I learned that to enjoy western-style homes in this place required maintaining a careful distance from the land. The lessons of my youth, odd enough in Los Angeles, seemed especially challenged here, near the Bering Sea. My new house was built on neither rock nor sand. It was built on air.

In historic times, the tribes of the Yukon-Kuskokwim Delta near the Bering Sea built semi-subterranean houses. The Yup'ik Eskimo lived partly in and partly out of the earth. During the coldest parts of the dark winters, they lived inside the land, burrowed into the ground for comfort, hunkered low beneath the howling winds off the Bering Sea, surrounded by insulating turfs of earth, heated by the flickering flames of seal-oil lamps. At spring breakup, the ice jammed-up the main rivers and flooded the wetlands, filling homes with frigid water. In this event they lived out of the ground, sitting atop their dwellings, waiting for the floods to recede. During the long daylights, families preferred skin tents and other airy shelters, moving from spring squirrel camps in the mountains to summer salmon camps along the rivers to fall berry camps on the low tundra. In my new house, I enjoyed no such intimacies with these northern lands. I floated above them.

I suffered badly that first year, all alone, adjusting to a new job and new world in that odd house. What was commonplace shocked my sensibilities, churned up my stomach. The house was designed so the sink's water poured through the drain hole straight to the tundra below. My dishwater did not disappear into a pipe that took it away to a sewage plant perched on a sand-dune bluff for dumping at sea out of sight and out of mind, as we did it in California. Here it cascaded directly down, kersplash, to the sand pad, freezing into a solid, milky glacier extending with the winter into the wetlands. I was offended by the sight of my own discharges, a slippery frozen stalagmite of accreted gray water, detergents, and food scraps, dumped right underfoot. In my house, the toilet was a five-gallon plastic bucket holding two fingers of disinfectant. I filled it weekly with a stinking brown sludge. But I refused to chuck it onto the nearest frozen pond as was customary for many of my neighbors. Instead, I paid for a weekly pickup, a service by barrel-chested workers in canvas overalls who chucked it for me onto a pond two miles away. This was more like we did it in California. I had water delivered to my house by truck. They filled her tanks like an automobile. The water was tea brown, an organic brew leached from the tundra. I learned that it exploded my plumbing whenever the town's power failed, freezing and bursting my pipes asunder. I returned from trips to carnage of busted pipes and hundreds of brown, frozen waterfalls. Once I entered my kitchen, breath condensing in the subzero air, to find my African violets flash frozen, as fresh-looking and brightly hued as when the power failed, transformed to delicate ice sculptures that disintegrated between my warm fingers. I visited my first gastrointestinal specialist, in Anchorage, that winter. He prescribed Mylanta for the culture shock.

That winter I lunched at the kitchen table, moping, staring out double-paned thermal windows to the tundra where my gray-water glacier crept outward inch by inch, wondering if I'd survive my first year. Unexpectedly, I noticed a diminutive old man bundled in a heavy parka and oversized pack boots, shuffling about the tussocks, drifts, and frosted willows. He was bent to the earth as if searching for lost keys. I noticed him coming and going over the span of weeks, wandering, bending, busy. Who was he? What was he doing outside my house? And then he was gone.

"You had a new neighbor," the Irish carpenter remarked one afternoon as I returned from work at the Fish and Game building. That day, unannounced, my landlord had begun framing another house in my driveway a few steps from my front door. "I can't park the truck," I said. "Don't worry," he replied. "I'll move it when I'm done." What could I say? It was his sand pad. He worked all winter on the house, and in spring it rented. When I departed Bethel for Juneau, that house still sat in the driveway.

My other neighbor, the mysterious old man I had watched through my window, had left. Curious, I explored where he'd been. I discovered he had excavated a semisubterranean house. It was a crawl hole leading down into a single small room scooped from the frozen earth, buttressed with scavenged lumber and roofed with blown plywood. Turfs of earth mounded over the frame provided insulation. He had modified an oil drum for burning wood, vented through the roof with stovepipe. After the early snows, the structure had become just another small mound on the tundra, blending completely with the land. He had lived there just a short while until he located relatives in town, said some of my other neighbors. They were from Nunivak Island, just off the Bering Sea coast directly west of Bethel. And they knew him because, like them, the old man was from the island, a hunter from a well-known family of carvers. Nunivak Island had emptied out, I learned. More of her people now lived away from the island than at Mekoryak, her last remaining village. Like a potato-blighted Ireland, Nunivak was sending her children off into the wider world. The old man was part of the flow, a newcomer in transitional housing, passing between worlds. In my unbalanced transitional state, I felt an instant kinship.

Bethel's a small town. Not surprisingly, we eventually met. He appeared one afternoon at the Fish and Game office, a short, wiry man dressed in rolled-up jeans, worn brown jacket splitting white at the seams, and a weathered billed cap. He smiled and lifted up a paper sack. "He has something to sell," the receptionist said. We were the last office in the building. He had been unsuccessful selling whatever it was.

From the bag he carefully lifted a small carving fashioned from wood, which he handed to me. It was the white face of a seabird. It carried a fish in its black,

hooked beak. Only its face could be seen. The bird was passing through the plane of a double hoop. Its body was as yet invisible, unrevealed, hidden within the dimension beyond the plane. Around the hoop, the old man had drilled holes for inserting pegs featuring feathers, more fish, and the head and feet of other creatures, items he removed from the sack. With pride, he showed me how to insert the pegs in the hoop encircling the seabird in the order he intended.

I held it complete in my hands. It was a Yup'ik mask of a type once worn in winter dances to honor the animals. The animals sustained the Yup'ik people with food and clothing and oil for heat. In a show of respect, the people donned masks, performing in midwinter ceremonies. Moving to the beat of walrus-gut drums, the masked dancers briefly became the animals, telling stories with the songs of the chorus, celebrating life, its seasons, and its abundance. Of course, the masked dancers weren't really animals. Pushing up the mask, the dancer revealed a face. There was a person beneath. And likewise, the ancient stories said this was true of the animals themselves. They were persons beneath, pushing up the pointed beaks and furry snouts. This was a Yup'ik truth about nature.

On Nunivak Island, missionaries of the Covenant Church banned dancing with masks sometime during the 1930s. The missionaries said the masks represented pagan images, honoring devilish spirits. In entreaties for help from animals, shamans dabbled with sorcery, consorting with familiars. Of all God's creations, only humans had souls, the missionaries claimed. Animals were animals. The people of Nunivak acquiesced to the missions. They destroyed their drums and dance fans. They drowned them in the sea. So began the century of the diaspora from Nunivak Island.

Yet history took an odd twist on Nunivak. The islanders continued to create masks. They didn't make them for dancing, they told the missionaries. They sculpted them for hanging on walls for sale to collectors and other visitors. The seabird mask I held in my hand had a small bent-nail hook on its back. The hook, it seemed, made the masks theologically acceptable. And as the men created, the carving of masks to honor animals reached new artistic heights on Nunivak Island. Their masks became widely known, acquired by museums and art collections. Like the placement of Bibles in every motel room, the carvers on Nunivak Island became the Gideons of the Yup'ik worldview, seeding their masks throughout the world, spreading truths about nature encoded in wood, if we can read them.

We hardly conversed about his mask of the seabird, the bird he carved passing between two worlds, the world we see and the world we do not. I cannot speak Yup'ik. He spoke little English. The bilingual secretary struggled with his island dialect. So our meeting was mainly smiles and appreciative gestures. This was enough. He sold me his mask, his Yup'ik model of the natural world, my first Gideon. We both were pleased. Before he left, he asked for a pen to sign the back of his work. He was Frank Shavings.

As a child I found it hard to see nature in Los Angeles. So much of it was blacktopped. Murky smog obscured the mountains. Dingy sand covered the cobbled beaches, dredged and pumped from offshore shoals and smoothed each morning by beach crews for the sunbathers. The developers contoured the hillsides, landscaped in ice plants, oleanders, and ornamental palms. As far as the eye could see stretched a sea of houses in mass-produced suburbs expanding to fill every level space. Nature was there, just hard to see. In Los Angeles, we knew of nature from the periodic earthquakes, hillside fires, and floods down the cemented arroyos. After the perky coverage on the evening news, the sun always rose to another mild, though somewhat hazy, day. We could find nature in the public parks reserved for that purpose. The Mojave, the Sierra, the redwoods, the sequoias, the Joshua trees, they were all freeway close. As a child, I first encountered nature in these set-aside parklands. But I first began to speak with nature in Alaska, directly atop my house in Juneau.

My Juneau house was a short walk from downtown. It had no stilts. The house sat solidly on a steep, rocky slope with about three dozen other small homes in the Behrends tract. Perhaps you've seen it on television. It's a subdivision of some notoriety for its location at the foot of majestic Mount Juneau, incomprehensibly situated at the tidewater end of a major avalanche chute. An avalanche special on TV featured our neighborhood. In this video show of nature's grandeur and irrepressible destructiveness, you can watch footage of a moderate-sized avalanche coming down the other side of Mount Juneau, momentarily erasing the capital city in a massive back draft of powdery fluff. You also can hear my neighbor being interviewed about why his family lived at the foot of a major slide path with a mean return interval of 14.4 years. His rationalizations are completely lame and entirely understandable to me. Like my slide-zone neighbor, I had made a personal covenant with the mountain. A rational person could not live there otherwise.

Before my commitment to this neighborhood, I found a vantage on Gastineau Channel, straight across from the avalanche chute, about a half mile as an Alaskan crow flies. I sought a better view of the mountain and the houses strung beneath it. Standing in the Behrends neighborhood itself I could not really see, craning my neck up the sweeping granite cliffs lost high above in the mists, like a flea inspecting the dog. To gain perspective, I stood on the beach across the channel. From there I could trace the shape of the slide path coming off the mountain. At the top was the place of the snow cornices, first piled up and then undercut by the fierce Taku winds of winter until their release by gravity. There the snow cascaded off a vertical drop. There it flowed down, taking out the forests. There it possibly diverted down a lateral ravine from right to left, racing at freight-train speeds. The paths of destruction split and widened near the mountain's base, slowed by the friction of accumulated debris, the mud, the boulders, and the ripped spruce, probably stopping just about there. To my eye, the house I could buy appeared to sit just outside the farthest edge of the eastern-most path. "I see you have spared my house," I spoke to the mountain. In this way, I began our thirteen-year conversation. I had acquired a new neighbor. A mountain. More precisely, the mountain had acquired me.

The bank demanded insured homes. I discovered that insurance companies offered nothing called avalanche insurance. "No problem," explained our realtor, who had sold many homes in the avalanche chutes. The insurers offered water insurance. And mud insurance. And wind insurance. What was an avalanche except some water, mud, and wind? With a wink and a warm handshake, the congenial banks sealed the deal. Against professional advice from many special committees, the city and borough of Juneau has refused to condemn this subdivision or to buy out the owners. Where would it stop, the municipal leaders asked? Most of Juneau sat atop slopes slipping toward the sea—in technical language, built atop "mass wasting zones," a wondrously vivid image. Juneau was not a society coddled by Big Brother governments. Alaska was the northern frontier, a great land of untamed nature, rugged individualism, and, apparently, caveat emptor.

I spoke with the mountain even before I learned that the Tlingits did too. They also were my new neighbors. In the southeast forests, the Tlingits spoke to glaciers, rivers, bears, halibut hooks, and many other things. For me, speaking to the mountain seemed natural, automatic. There was the mountain and here were we. My second wife, Sylvia, and two young children, the family I loved, were joined at the hip with the mountain, a part of something great and entirely uncontrollable. And I discovered the mountain spoke back. The winds roared through the spruce. The rivers cascaded down the mountain's face. The eagles screamed and whistled, soaring about their dead snags. The rains pelted down consistently, gathered by the mountain's massive walls from the ocean's mists. Continuously, the mountain spoke back, season by season. A hundred miles of hard-rock tunnels honeycombed the mountain, remnants of Juneau's gold rush. At times I stood at the black mouths of the adits feeling the mountain breathe, great cold breaths expelled from the deeps, blowing sweet and powerfully around me. The mountain grew more alive with every year I lived, nested with my family on the mountain's slope. And in this way I grew to know a new kind of love. In the clear winter's silence, after the hurricane of storms off the ice fields, I would lean at my doorstep, staring up to the white snow cornices hanging high above our heads, and talk with the mountain wearing them, as a bride wears tatted-silk veils. "You are dangerously beautiful today," I would say. In her silence, I knew she loved to hear it.

Above my newest home, the small citrus trees I planted last fall have died. I'm not sure why. Citrus does not grow in Alaska, so I never tried. But citrus trees are supposed to thrive here in my newest home, San Marcos, California, a small, burgeoning community at the northernmost edge of San Diego County, about a hundred miles south of the bean fields where I was almost born. We moved in

2001, my family and I. Sylvia was ecstatic to be warm once again. My daughter cried. My son shrugged. And I began wondering about the course of human life. It appears my life has turned full circle, a journey with the same beginning as end, an unsettling circuit. But I discover I'm not the same person who sailed off on that northbound ferry two decades before. And California is not the same world I left. I am rediscovering this mythic land.

I know so little about citrus or that slope above my house or the bugs that may have attacked them. The leaves shriveled and dropped and the wood gave up. Perhaps I planted too deeply for the rocky ground that seems to hold water like a bucket, drowning them in my lean rations. So I'm trying again. This time I've planted the saplings higher off the rock, in a mound of mulch, cobble, and sand. I've smeared their thin trunks with a sticky gum to discourage the ants from carrying livestock into the canopies, their aphids and honey scales. I don't begrudge the ants their husbandry, but not in these fragile striplings. We'll see how this works, the trees and I, whether an orange, a grapefruit, and a former Alaskan are right for this place.

Most of my newest neighbors are ants. They dominate by any measure —sheer numbers, total biomass, or economic enterprise. I've heard that, by weight, ants comprise 30 percent of all terrestrial creatures. I believe it's possible. Our house sits atop a massive anthill. More precisely, because these are ants that erect nothing, it's built atop subterranean colonies that, I'm told, continuously extend for hundreds of miles beneath California, from Sandy Bagels to Frisco.

San Marcos is a place of little valleys, coastal chaparral, and smallholder orchards. The housing developers are rapidly filling it up with new tract homes. Kaiser's dream lives on in California. The homes are still mass-produced with respectable amenities, as Kaiser originally directed, but there is no longer any pretense about affordability. In this place median houses sell for obscene amounts, and I wonder, how do Californians afford it? There must be vast hidden wealth or deeply entrenched debt in this new California. Probably both. The developers have scraped and contoured the little valleys and planted them with red-tiled, two-story homes all in rows, much like the growers have done with the avocados. They most certainly did not consult the ants. The ants hail from Argentina. Argentine ants, I have learned, are recent immigrants to California, just like my family and most of my other neighbors. We are building the new world order here together. So many of us are exotics, I wonder what will take root and what will mysteriously wither.

The new California encourages carpools, a thing started just before I left. They provide special lanes on most freeways and their on-ramps, enticements to gridlocked commuters to please share their wheeled homes with just one other person, the traffic's so bad. But it's still almost uniformly single heads during rush-hour commutes. I'm a driver in a daily carpool to and from San Marcos High School. The school eliminated bus service during last year's budget cuts. There's plenty of time to chat during the jam-ups around campus.

We're an all-Californian carpool. Each afternoon I transport a Filipino, a Laotian, and an Alaskan. This is typical. It's a multicultural, polyglot high school, drawn from a community holding its second annual multicultural festival in the park this Sunday, last year's being so successful. We're especially rich with Hispanic students recently arrived from poorer regions like Michoacán, Oaxaca, Zacatecas, and San Luis Potosí. Many, maybe most, have hardworking parents who border crossed in the secret blacks of night, drawn to the promised land. Multiculturalism is the fact of California's present and the hope of California's future. We've just elected an Austrian to be governor, a grinning, body-building movie star who effusively shouts, "That's fantastic!" What better icon for the new California transforming with the influx of exotics, all of us making passage to an emerging world, setting our roots together, hoping we've not dug ourselves in too deep.

In our carpool, my Filipino rider gabs about kidnappers. This is a great familial worry, so pressing that her parents directed her brother to chop down the trees beside their house, the tall ones above the red-tiled roof, to remove routes of access. They pray for home security to icons of Jesus and Mary enshrined in and outside their house. After school, my rider is secured under lock and key at home. She's carefully chaperoned in public. My daughter's freedom of movement impresses her, coming and going as she pleases—how kids do it in Alaska, I explain. I also ask her to please not lock the car doors when she exits. "Just another Alaskan habit," I say. She looks incredulous. No locked car doors! But she quickly learns my funny ways of doing things. Another day kidnappers sneak into the conversation again. "San Marcos is likely among the safest places on the planet for young women," I say to her. She's thinking about it.

My Laotian rider's worries are no less ephemeral. Her family is dealing with ghosts in their house, just a few blocks from ours. A ghost child has recently appeared in her dreams. The child occasionally materializes on the upstairs landing. "All houses come with ghosts," explains the old grandmother who lives with them. Even ten-year-old California tract homes. "What will you do," I ask?

"The Buddha helps with ghosts," my young rider explains. But the Buddha in their house's shrine must be kept informed. The family has fallen short. The Buddha knew nothing of a cousin's recent arrival or sudden departure. The house became disturbed. The ghosts appeared.

We've brought our house icons too. Two woodblock prints by Charles Rohrbacher, Juneau's iconographer for the Russian Orthodox Church, are installed in our living room—the *Fifth Day of Creation*, showing the Creator awhirl in fish and birds, and *Jesus Washing the Disciples' Feet*, one of the Brethren's odder rites, except we kneel to do it. In bending him at the waist, Charles hasn't got Jesus quite right, at least to Brethren thinking. In our glass cabinet sits a heavy copper printing plate from the Brethren Press, black with dried ink from pressing out thousands of page 27 for the old Brethren hymnal. Etched in bold relief, it reads backward, "Joyful, Joyful We Adore Thee," Beethoven's *Ninth*, a favorite. A garish yellow-orange cross from San Miguel de Allende in Mexico hangs above our fireplace, studded with glass marbles shining like raindrops over cutout paper portraits of tiny people. It supports green ivy that can't stop growing. Unfortunately, none of these seems as good as the Buddha in our neighbor's place. That's a fact, at least for what troubles our new home. Not kidnappers or ghosts. Argentine ants.

A recent houseguest disagreed one night at our dinner table. He was a country minister from West Virginia, part of the Brethren Disaster Response Team responding to massive wildfires that tore through the region's chaparral last fall, devastating nearby families. We hosted him for two weeks while he volunteered in a children's daycare. "In the book of Genesis," he pronounced, "we are given authority over the animals." He realized that this is an astonishing claim, but he personally tested it at youth camp one year by charging the mosquitoes not to bite him in the name of the Creator. At the week's end his arms were smooth and untouched, though the arms of the other campers were red and bumpy. We politely listened to this demonstration of man and nature. Then with her mischievous smile my daughter offered to interpret it. "You charged the mosquitoes to bite everyone else," she explained. He looked stunned. Then he slapped his thigh, guffawing heartily. We plunged back into the friendly theological disagreements, going long into the evening, Eastern and Pacific Slope Brethren, old-fart ministers and obstreperous daughters, all peas in the same pod.

In our house is an as-yet-unresolved dispute between humans and ants over occupancy and use. The house icons expect the disputants themselves to peaceably settle it. As I see things, probably the ants have some legitimate prior claim.

They were residents before the housing development, even if only by a few years. When we arrived, the ants clearly were house occupants. They had established customary use of most rooms. This included built-ins like the electrical outlets and conduits, the closets, the kitchen cabinets and drawers, the bathroom medicine chests, the microwave oven (even when on), and the dishwasher (foraging by the thousands between wash cycles). However, their occupancy and use of items we've since installed, such as (but not limited to) the potted plants, the cat's dish, the refrigerator, the hand mixer, the steam iron, the digital piano, and the computer are clearly invasive. And disruptive. My children cannot play the piano with ants popping from the keys. Nor can I type essays on a colonized laptop spewing a succession of ants onto the thumb pad. And regardless of any prior claims, we've purchased the place. The sizable down and the signatures with the bank are ours, not theirs.

Negotiating with ants is more than just difficult. It's nearly impossible. They are so extremely numerous and decentralized, it's hard to know who to negotiate with. They are extraordinarily expansive, establishing new colonies overnight as though this were a natural right, making points of contention rapidly moving targets. They overwhelm all competition, the indigenous ants, bees, wasps, and even (I'm told) birds, eliminating our natural allies in the dispute. And most egregious, they ignore us completely. They treat us as epiphenomena. The principal problem with their modus operandi is eminently clear: the ants are acting altogether too human.

North County offers entire industries devoted to solving my dispute with the ants. They market chemical solutions. If the tract developers and pest control companies aren't branches of corporate conglomerates, someone's probably looking into it. The pest control promoters want to sell me scorched-earth policies. For a monthly fee, sprayers in protective breathing masks will treat my whole property, searching and destroying each and every ant colony, wasp nest, beehive, spiderweb, and most probably, bird nest or bunny warren. I ask the promoter, "What about my herb garden, the second-year grapes, and the citrus saplings?" "Oh, safe, safe." Fruits from the poisoned earth are safe. "But keep the cat indoors and cover her water dish for, um . . . four hours is safe enough," the promoter affirms. I ask, "What about the fate of the volatiles that progressively leap northward with the sun and wind, season by season, year by year, for final deposition in the fats of high-end food-chain animals like harbor seals and beluga whales, hunted by my northern friends?" The bug man doesn't know what I'm babbling about. Another greenie. What's California coming to, he wonders. And so do I.

At present I see few simple solutions. A friend recommends borax in sugar that the ants carry away to selectively destroy their colonies. Maybe it will come to that. But instead I'm trying a good-neighbor policy. We will explore living civilly side by side, like good neighbors should. I'll not search and destroy their colonies. But the colonies should not extend inside the house (or up the new citrus). "It's a 'leaky boat' program," I tell my kids. Imagine the house is our boat in a sea of ants. We simply find and plug all leaks. Cinnamon, soap suds, masking tape, petroleum jelly, wood putty, spot sprays of insecticides, hairy resident spiders, we use them all, depending on nook or crack. We're pure eclectics. Collectively they're intended to convey messages to the ant colony outside. This route is closed. This way is nasty foul. This corridor is certain death. This barrier marks the start of another's territory. We are several months into the program. I'm confident that the colonies still care little about us humans, they are that self-absorbed. But by all indications their morning patrols are correctly reading the new road signs. They are beginning to leave the house alone. We are becoming better neighbors.

Despite the massive urban growth, there's something I have noticed in the new California that I didn't as a youth, sliding on coastal sand dunes covered with ice plant: nature is easier to see. No doubt I'm seeing with different eyes. Many of us are. The mountains loom clearer above the flat basin that cradles Los Angeles. The air smells better, I think. "Buy cheap gas here!" shouts a sign at the Arizona border to California-bound drivers—"$.34 per gallon cheaper!" It's true. The additives to California's gasoline to help it burn cleaner and clearer, required by the laws passed by her citizens' representatives, are expensive. Gasoline supplies ran short last week in San Marcos as refineries switched between winter and summer blends, briefly spiking up costs by 20 percent. I'm glad to see it. If they go still higher, the new Sprinter train line being built through San Marcos may receive more political support and future riders. Maybe they'll install two carpool lanes.

Agua Hedionda drains the little valley by my home, flowing just two blocks away toward the sea, sparkling in the distance. Its Spanish name means "stinky water," contrasting with Buena Creek, the neighboring watershed. Our little creek exploded with croaky frogs last week following a week of winter monsoons. I'm glad we live two long blocks away. And I'm glad they're croaking. This year, a grassroots group passed out brochures door to door to keep the watershed undeveloped.

Agua Hedionda forms a lagoon just before entering the Pacific Ocean. In 2000 the lagoon saw its own frightening explosion of a green tropical algae called *Caulerpa taxifolia*, sold as a decorative aquarium plant. This same algae, accidentally released, is devouring portions of the Mediterranean Sea, blanketing its bottom with a sterile monoculture of destruction, vast uniform mats like Astroturf. Apparently someone emptied a fishbowl into Agua Hedionda or rinsed one out by a storm drain. Something as simple as that, and the lagoon was infected. An escape of the tiny algae from the lagoon threatened to destroy California's rich coastal ecosystems. But it wasn't allowed to escape. Remarkably, someone spotted the new exotic, small and underwater. Nature is more visible in the new California. The last several years, plot by plot, contract divers have squirted chlorine beneath tarps framed with PVC pipe, moving carefully along the lagoon's bottom, a slow, laborious, low-tech solution taking several efforts to kill the intruder without hurting the lagoon. The papers cover the effort as front-page news, and Californians pack conventions on *Caulerpa taxifolia*. Working with nature seems no longer confined to parklands or paid professionals; it's common enterprise.

I couldn't live in Los Angeles anymore, I tell myself. It's now too congested, too expensive, too hectic: someone else's cup of tea. My childhood home has transformed into another world. I drove to her airport recently to gather up a troop of Girl Scouts from Alaska, all giddy to hit the white beaches. As the plane was delayed, I toured my old haunts. I observed that the cheap stucco houses that Kaiser built for my parents' generation have gone through multiple remodels. I hardly recognized my childhood home, nor could I afford it today. The avocado planted by my grandfather is still there. Maybe it still produces fruit.

On the coastal fringes of my childhood's world, the Pacific waters still stretch out like flattened steel. The jets still roar overhead, minute by minute, exporting California's dreams to other worlds. But beneath the flight path, through the mesh of tall chain-link fencing, I discover an unexpected desolation. The beach homes perched on the coastal ridge are gone, razed, removed, leaving only a testament of decaying gray foundations among dry weed patches aglitter with broken glass. The remnants whisper to me of childhood lessons. Lives built on sand. On this stretch of paradise, ever-expansive runways, flight schedules, and noise finally became insufferable to human life. The beach homeowners sued. A consuming legal fight ensued between neighbors with an inevitable outcome. The beach homes lost out to the planes, the eminent domain of inexorable progress. They were bought out, boarded up, bulldozed.

But then the unexpected unfolded. They were the wings of the El Segundo Blue butterfly. When the airport's plans for a recreational area and twenty-seven-hole golf course on the emptied dunes went public, California's public rose up in protest. The tiny, overlooked butterfly was now listed as endangered, among the first under the Endangered Species Act, a law passed in 1973 by America's representatives who were beginning to see nature, even in Los Angeles. In 1985, following a second long battle, the airport's plans for the dunes were rejected by the California Coastal Commission, scrapped for something better. The ancient dunes, momentarily forgotten and almost lost beneath our feet, began to be uncovered once again. At present, a small, local nonprofit oversees weekend treks through the dunes by volunteers. They are slowly weeding and replanting with native varieties like the coastal buckwheat. The children among them eagerly look for legless lizards slithering in the sand.

Much has been lost. The butterflies and lizards have endured, but, sadly, the indigenous ants have perished. The Argentine ants have replaced them. Naturally. Yet I understand the Argentine ants have assumed their predecessors' traditional role of protecting butterflies. The exotic ants now watch over the larvae, the vulnerable caterpillars grazing on the coastal buckwheat. The ants harvest honeydew the larvae produce and guard them from predators. It's a mutually beneficial relationship. Evidently even these humanlike ants can learn to fill a cooperative niche. In the humble dunes twixt city and sea, the blue butterflies are coming back.

Alaska visitors like the Girl Scout troop always bring news from the North. "Look at the *Delta Discovery*," the troop leader told me, a small weekly paper covering the Yukon-Kuskokwim Delta. "There's an interesting story." I did. In December 2002, dancing resumed on Nunivak Island. The first dancing since 1937. The remarkable decision followed years of hard self-reflection within the community. Much had been forgotten. But fifteen precious songs had been preserved in a videotaped interview with a Nunivak elder just before he passed away, in 1999. Drum designs could be re-created from photographic records. Such fragments were enough. Mekoryak invited Tununak and Toksook Bay, neighboring mainland villages, to the three-day celebration at its school gymnasium. The invited villages danced first. And then the nervous Nunivak dancers followed, performing the first song danced by the Yup'iks of Nunivak in sixty-five years. At its end came thunderous applause. In the ensuing silence, a single voice cried out, Pamyua! Again!

In my patch of the new California earth, I notice that the succulents in the sandy spots are bursting with growth after the recent weeklong drenching, like nearby Stinky Creek with its squiggling tadpoles. They seem much happier than the citrus, extruding strange stalks, hanging out elongated flowers and weird, fruiting buds. Some of the succulents came by way of my sweet sister, who visits us from her place beneath those mountains to the north, the ones emerging from the haze. Others I lifted from my mother-in-law's place, a stone's throw away in San Marcos. But on the stony slope where I've built my new life, the red apple yellows and fails. The groundcover is not happy in this place, scraped from the hillside by the industrialists for the house, exposing a type of ground never there before. The slope lists, steep and hot, nearly impermeable with its thin, almost nonexistent topsoil. It's clearly killing these transplants, the red apple and the citrus. But I've recently noticed a nursery now dealing in native California plants. Maybe a native plant would like this rocky patch of earth, a hardy bunch grass, a manzanita, a stickery chaparral. I'll search for something there. Or maybe on my next stroll along Stinky Creek, croaking with its latest batch of frogs, perhaps I'll discover it there, that perfect transplant, surrounding us still, simply diminished and momentarily forgotten, a part of life taken back, waiting for us, already suited for new solid rock.

2  Humanity

Cautionary Tales of Near-Death and

Transformation for the Lost

Don't imagine it's always possible for the lost to find the way home.
There are powerful currents and tides. And even at the slack you can find yourself waist deep in the cold, searching for channels with a gray horizon clamped
down like a pot lid. I have learned it's not easy. It's no easy matter in the dark of
winter, when the ice ruptures and the sea overflows to know even where to step.
Or how to cross the pressure ridges when your feet are dead, your very tears
frozen, and you are alone. There are times when the icy winds whistle through
the tall, frozen grasses like dead voices, calling this way, this way, but no matter
which way you turn, it's in your face. Lie down on the ground when the winds
blow false, they say. Lie down flat. But then the only voice heard is your own
self-deception. Lying lost and alone in an empty place, I have come to learn
this. The way home will not be by the trail you blaze but by paths set by others.

Bethel—also called Mamterillaq, "site of many caches"—is a regional center
in western Alaska near the Bering Sea somewhat below the Arctic Circle. As
shown by its Yup'ik name, this is a place with food, a place of humanity, about
five thousand people when I lived there. Its cluster of buildings thrust up from
the tundra, much like tiny filaments of lichen on a vast glacial till. It's a substantial place to humans. But from a bird's-eye view, Bethel is quickly lost among
trackless miles of tundra and meandering sloughs where the Yukon and Kuskokwim rivers have left a great delta before entering the sea. In winter it breathes
a fine smoke of filmy life across a black-and-white mosaic, soon absorbed by the

gray vastness. Snowmachines lay spiderwebbed traces about her, icy connections to more distant villages.

I'll start with two stories from Bethel, for it was there that certain paths began for me, but I'll end with events near the foot of Denali, where I gained a clearer view. The first is an account of a lost Yup'ik child and the second, a lost cat named Sam. As I consider them today, I wonder if they are the same story. At the time I had not connected them at all. They are lessons about humanity, cautionary tales of near-death and transformation for all who are lost. They are about crossing fragile lines. They hold mysteries I'm still working through. The one event, the lost child, remains bewildering. It reaches beyond my experience and encapsulates for me a fundamental dissonance, except for the other, the lost cat, which I saw for myself. The stories may be told in any order, I think, parallel translations from a common text. But I'll begin chronologically with the lost child, the sadder tale. I heard it my first year in Bethel. For those more familiar with events, please forgive my errors.

The lost child was a Yup'ik boy born in a tundra village. There are three, Atmautluak, Kasigluk, and Nunapitchuk, nestled on the low, soggy banks of the inner delta far from roads. He was a simpleton. The small village could offer no special services for the developmentally delayed. So, hoping for the best, his family placed the boy in a school at Bethel, a residential facility for students with special needs, located near the town's center.

As is common for Yup'iks boarded at schools, the child fell sick for home. So he escaped. Incautiously, repeatedly, he fled the school. They retrieved him several times, always putting him back. But at last, during winter, he escaped completely. He fled west across the flat tundra. "He's running home," they said, forty miles, straight line. A search-and-rescue was launched. But as the days passed he was not found. He did not find home. He was lost.

This simple tragedy then takes a disconcerting turn. Travelers begin to see him, or think they do. It's always from a distance. Their calls rebuffed, he bolts and hides. He's fast. "It's the boy, his clothes tattered with wear," they say. How is it possible in the cold without food? "He's a village boy," they say. "He's catching food beneath the ice, whitefish, pike, and blackfish. Gathering last fall's berries frozen on bushes in sheltered places. Snaring ptarmigan and hares. Snatching animals hobbled by drifts." There's great skepticism. And some are alarmed. They do not like to hear these things. Don't worry, others say. It happens. He won't hurt you. He's only searching for home.

With the stretch of winter, the sightings persist. The boy has grown. He's bigger, some say very big, larger than a man. His clothes have weathered away. He's now covered with furs. He looks like a giant, hairy man. He's exceptionally fast, outpacing snowmachines, and exceedingly clever, appearing and disappearing in an eye blink. There's a Yup'ik name for what he's become: *aarayu-lit*—screamers. The old name affirms that this happens.

The account ends poignantly. At long last he finds his way home. One night he appears in the village of his childhood. They hear him crunching on the snow among the houses, crying with happiness. He begins to sing. To him he sings words of joy. To the villagers, it's like the sound of a wolf singing to the sky.

Returning from Alaska to my own childhood home, reentering the culture and way of life in southern California, it became clearer to me how I had profoundly changed. I could sense it, feel it, change as certain as age. It had been twenty years, after all. I was balder from that maternal chromosome (they say), smarter with experience (I believe). Yet this was not what I sensed. What I mean to say is, it seemed as if I had been changed *because* of the North. Changed because I had been in the Far Northern parts of this world and nowhere else. Changed in ways that could not have happened had I lived those same years on a Seattle sound, or a Topeka plain, or a Manhattan tarmac. They were subtle, incontrovertible, close-to-the-skin changes that I felt like my sweat when the others around me pulled on light jackets.

Do you believe this? Is it possible that each of us has no personal program triggered at birth by familial genes (or celestial ascensions) to run a preset course? Is it possible, or perhaps even standard, that persons are launched along alternate trajectories by precise moments, places, and peoples, turning into one thing substantially different from another? Like a great uncle of mine who had whiffed mustard gas in World War I. After that moment, he claimed he was never again quite the same person. I remember the phrase he used—never again quite the same person. Had I been changed like that? By a whiff of something from the North?

Maybe we were all huffing something with Sam, the cat. The second story is his. Sam was a neighbor's housecat. At the time this was somewhat special. Unlike humans and dogs, tabby cats were recent imports to Bethel. There were not many compared with the dogs, who have lived with Yup'iks for several thousand years. There's but one indigenous cat on the Yukon-Kuskokwim Delta occasionally trapped in the uplands for its beautifully mottled, fragile pelt during high rabbit cycles—the lynx.

It's pure digression to note that some Yup'iks will eat a lynx, but most do not. The lynx sits on the cusp of what is considered *food* and *not food*. It sits in the company of a handful of other in-between animals, such as minks and gulls. Though some consider them a delicacy, minks are hard to eat because of the strong musky flavor. Some hang mink carcasses outdoors at length, but even then it's more than most can take. Gull *eggs* are regularly eaten but usually not the gulls themselves, except maybe on St. Lawrence Island. Unlike most other large birds on the delta—the geese and sea ducks, the cranes and swans, the dabbling ducks and snowy owls, all eagerly hunted—gulls are usually left alone. It was explained to me that if I should ever recover the body of a drowned person, I would know why gulls are usually not eaten. Some won't eat shrimp for the same reason. What puts lynx on the culinary fence is less certain to me. Someone said it had to do with the eyes, how they stare at you. I don't understand this yet.

Housecats had a hard time in Bethel. Dogs regularly killed them. When I lived there, mushers staked their sled dogs near the margins of town. They posed little threat to a cat with any sense. The main danger were housedogs loose and running in packs. Many families kept a dog chained near the house as an all-purpose pet, watchdog, and scrap disposal. Unfortunately for everyone, loose dogs were a menace. To keep strays under control, once or twice a year the city announced a shoot. My neighbor's Sam was kept indoors because of this. Sam was her beautiful prize, sleek, shorthair, sporting fine bars of grays and whites. He displayed all the endearing cat traits, rubbing legs, head butting, purring, sleeping, and sitting on the kitchen sill for hours watching the world. He was let out once a day to do his business.

Then one afternoon Sam disappeared. He was simply gone. Friends searched without success. Winter came and Sam's keeper sadly conceded the inevitable, dogs had killed him, or the subzero weather. Now my wife tells me cats sometimes do this. They walk away, never to return. She has had a series of cats and has buried a few. She counts them off—Goldie (old age), Socks (killed by dogs), Max (poisoned), and Cinnamon (old age). But Rabbit, El Tigre, and the twins Foggy and Smoggy just disappeared. I learned these cat facts later. In Bethel, I knew little of cats. Sam was duly missed, briefly mourned, and quickly forgotten, the lot of cats outside ancient Egypt. In spring my neighbor adopted a new kitten, a tiny, smoke-colored thing, cute and playful. About then the sightings began.

It was difficult to believe, but people began to see Sam. He was ranging in another neighborhood, they said. He wouldn't come when called. He ran, hid, overly suspicious, exceptionally fast. "Come on," said his owner. How could he have survived the winter? Stealing. Handouts. Squeezed beneath the newer homes atop their pilings. My neighbor was skeptical. This didn't sound like Sam. "He was gray like Sam," they said. There are few gray cats around. But it was larger than Sam, much larger. He had grown. He was covered with thick, thick fur.

When the mystery peaked, I visited my neighbor. She had gone to see for herself. Sure enough, there was a cat under the houses. And it came when she called. She was visibly nervous, letting me in, clutching her new kitten. "Look," she whispered, nodding toward the living room. I must truthfully confess I could hardly believe it. There was something exceptional asleep on her couch. It was huge, as large a cat or catlike animal as I had ever seen or thought possible inside a house, more like a lynx. Its hair was long, thickly matted, interwoven with dry grass and other detritus, pressed and ratted into massive felt protruding from all sides like protective armor, as broad as a badger. This was Sam? "Are you sure," I whispered? "Yes," she replied unsurely. It knew her. It knew the place. "But that was not all," she whispered back. Sam had changed in other ways. How he moved, or rather stalked around the house. How he voiced, cougarlike. She shuddered and hugged the kitten. Just then Sam roused, yawned, and stretched his great body, opening to us huge unblinking eyes that jumped with a wild flicker.

The notices she posted around town read, "Free cat to a good home." My neighbor lost hope after a week. "People take one look," she said, "and that's it." Understandably. Who'd want a cat like this? But we were forgetting about Yup'iks. They knew even less about cats than I did. Sam's fate took an unexpected turn when a family from one of the tundra villages, in town for shopping, read the notice. They came to inspect Sam and were absolutely delighted. That's the kind of cat we've been looking for, they exclaimed! They had tried cats before, but they seemed to get killed by dogs. No dog's going to bother that cat, they declared. The last report of Sam has him in a carrier aboard a skiff surrounded by his Yup'ik redeemers, heading for home down the Kuskokwim River.

As I've said, housecats are recent imports to western Alaska, so there may be no Yup'ik name for Sam's transformation. But there is in English, a language reaching back to old Eurasia, where humans first domesticated nature. It's *feral*, a domesticate that has reverted to an untamed state. What happens to cats (and other domesticates) is recurrent enough for a name. The word derives from an ancient Indo-European root, *ghwer-*, or wild beast, the root for other modern English words like *ferocious* and *fierce*. Through its Greek form, *ther*, are built the names of ancient monsters, like Dinothere and Megatherium. It seems Sam had "reverted" to a wild beast. He had reclaimed a hidden potential in cats, an undomesticated form waiting for release by proper conditions. Lost and alone in the Far North, he had transformed.

As his transformed self, Sam may even yet be terrorizing dogs in the tundra villages, for all I know. If so, he lives among good company. In western Alaska there are feral reindeer in several places—the Kilbuck Mountains south of the Kuskokwim and the Andreafsky Mountains south of Norton Sound. They are escapees from herds the government introduced from Siberia to Alaska in the late nineteenth century in a benevolent experiment to improve the social conditions of "starving" Eskimo. They have become almost like caribou, report Yup'iks who see them while hunting. Elsewhere in Alaska are other truants. I'm told there are shaggy feral cattle on Cherni, Dolgoi, and the Sanak Islands in the Aleutian chain that are hunted like the aggressive wild kine of old. Bison roam the upper Kuskokwim and the Copper River Basin east of the river, introduced from Montana early last century. Musk oxen brought from Greenland scare off migrating caribou, to the annoyance of Inupiat hunters. After nearly a century, the Kodiak brown bears still haven't figured out what to do with the black-tailed deer milling about on Kodiak Island, all descended from transplants. Should we eat them? The state of Alaska now officially frowns on such unnatural experiments. Government claims more sensitivity to the potentially monstrous effects of relocated life. State laws now prohibit transplanted animals such as mongoose, lions, and elephants. Imagine. Elephants, once again loosed in the North!

As a recent transplant to Southern California, I can subjectively attest to one annoying change: I hold no truck for traffic lights. Among other subtle internal changes, I find this entirely new and exasperating. To tell the truth, growing up in the Los Angeles basin I recall no feelings whatever toward traffic lights. Traffic lights were so commonplace they were simply another normal, almost natural feature of human life. Of course—traffic lights. But the cause of this new aversion is understandable.

My home is here in San Marcos, a modest but burgeoning town north of San Diego with 54,977 people, according to the recent federal census. Los Vallecitos de San Marcos was the original Spanish land grant—the Little Valleys of Saint Mark. The little valleys are covered with coastal chaparral. The temperatures are perfection, a microclimate from being precisely set inland from the Pacific to catch the daily exchanges of mountain and sea. The marine layer burns off by midmorning to gloriously mild days and clear, cool evenings, day after day after day. As I type this, it has not rained in substantial amounts for 183 days and counting.

My old home was in Juneau, the modest and beautiful capital city in Alaska's southeast archipelago, with 30,711 people. Juneau was named after Joe Juneau, who, with his partner, Richard Harris, was directed there for placer gold by Kowee, a local Tlingit clan head. According to lore, Joe and Richard were such drunks they misplaced the creek and had to be shown again. Each founder is buried side by side in the cemetery a short stroll from my old house beneath the breathtaking sweep of mountains above town. Kowee's immolation site is commemorated nearby. Juneau town clings to a narrow coastal bench sandwiched between the North Pacific and massive ice fields. The islands and mainland are covered with verdant, temperate rainforest. Downtown Juneau received about 85 inches of rain the year we departed, roughly seven feet of water.

Hold your laughs, but in Juneau, Alaska's capital city, there are thirteen traffic lights. At least there were the year we left. I can sit here and count them in my head. Their names are revealing. There was a light at the bridge, at Main, Salmon Creek, Lemon Creek, K-Mart, the mall, the airport, Egan-and-Mendenhall Glacier, the other mall (two there), Back Loop, Riverside Drive, and Engineer's Cutoff. There were none on Douglas Island, none in Thane, none out the road. Everywhere else it was stop signs, I think. This means that even if you worked hard at it, it was difficult to get stopped by traffic lights during a daily drive. A coffee run by car, essential in my line of work, took a scant few minutes.

In my new San Marcos home, a slightly bigger town, there are sixty-eight traffic lights, not thirteen. This will be an underestimate as I probably overlooked some while driving around yesterday with my eleven-year-old, who marked the map in his lap; more are installed each month. We counted ten alone between my home office and the nearest good cup of coffee, ten traffic lights in what may be a straight-line distance of less than three miles. On the mornings I hit most of the ten, which seems less than extraordinary during the preternatural morning traffic flows, sometimes I do more than just count them. I sit and fume and remember coffee runs in Juneau. On the very bad morning when traffic crawls between lights at an average stop of a minute each (including left-turn signals and time extensions triggered by commuter volume and the times you don't get through on one light), that's ten minutes—ten minutes of just sitting behind a steering wheel, doing nothing except waiting for a green light in order to crawl to the next. I ask you, comparing Juneau and San Marcos, which seems normal and natural to you? Now you may laugh.

Humanity is stretched thin across Alaska, particularly in areas like the Yukon-Kuskokwim Delta. If one divides its people by its land, a common preoccupation of demographers, Alaska boasts 1 person per square mile. For the Yukon-Kuskokwim Delta, it's something like 0.4 persons per square mile. This is thin compared with more southerly states like Illinois (223 persons per square mile), New York (402 persons), or New Jersey (1,134 persons). Big sky Montana is 6 times denser at six persons per square mile. Even in Anchorage, Alaska's largest urban center, people rattle around like peas in a bottle. Its density is only 153 persons per square mile, a poor joke compared with southern metropolises such as San Diego (3,772 persons per square mile), Los Angeles (7,877 persons), and (hold your hat) New York City (26,403 persons). My own little San Marcos shows a density of 2,314 persons per square mile, which may help explain its sixty-odd lights and daily traffic snarls. People are packed by northern standards.

But they say statistics can lie, especially averages, and this is true with densities. The thinness of Alaska's population as measured by average densities expresses only a potential, a distribution if all Alaskans were mysteriously and equally repellent. Which is the lie. In actuality, Alaska's human population is not thinly stretched across the landscape. It's clumped up. Most Alaskans choose to live in clumps—villages, towns, and small cities—with expansive open space between. The humans of the Far North congregate.

The isolated homestead is rare on the northern frontier. This is the case despite the self-sufficient yearnings that yank American heartstrings. Alaska has had its share of land stampedes. In the past century Alaskans have regularly competed for remote parcels offered up by the state. But visit the plots after ten years to see the number abandoned as permanent homesites. Self-reliant families braving the northern wilds in log cabins—such groups come and go with a frail, ghostlike beauty, ephemeral dissipations of human life, each with its romantic but tragic tale. The solitary homestead rates among the least successful of northern adaptations. Alaska Natives understood this long ago. There's a singular problem with the remote homestead—it doesn't hold enough people. It's not a desirable permanent arrangement. Among northern Native peoples, seasonal disbanding to effectively fish and hunt is commonly a valued necessity, but the general social rule is to clump up to survive. There's a critical mass for humanity.

Not enough people. It's a hard concept to even imagine, raised in Los Angeles. It has almost become an unknowable state since human populations have everywhere exploded. Green revolutions, penicillin, industrialization, and other advances have erased from memory a condition known well to our forebears—an insufficiency of people. We now know *more than enough people* and increasingly *way more than enough.* Among six and a quarter billion. It's rare to experience a dearth, and rarer to receive instruction about *not enough.*

But in Bethel I began to learn that the Far North offers courses in human insufficiency. The cultural knowledge was embedded in ancient names like *aarayulit* and *ghwer.* To a southern in-migrant like me, the words and their ancient lessons were no longer fresh or familiar. Within the global human surfeit, it was becoming forgotten knowledge. I discovered in the North it was still taught. The lessons were revealed by the unlucky, the sundered, and the lost— not every year, yet with a frequency to keep fed the northern people's longstanding awe of and unease with solitary life.

I first saw the personal torment of a solitary human on the Tonzona River, upriver from Bethel about three hundred miles. It was writ on the face of a man stranded by circumstance in a beautiful and empty land. He called to us from the riverbank to please stop the boat, join him for coffee, give him some news. I remember the discomfort of the boat driver and the pleading madness in the eyes of the abandoned.

We were looking for traditional salmon fish trap sites that day, sites for traps that had disappeared two decades before. The Tonzona is a remote tributary in the upper Kuskokwim drainage. The river flows near the western foothills of the Denali massif, a geologic protrusion from colliding plates in central Alaska containing the highest points in North America. By quirk of natural ecology, there are few places more empty of people than this piece of earth. It's a hungry place. The hardy salmon that make it from the North Pacific to the headwaters of the Kuskokwim River to spawn are exhausted, long spent of oil and few in number. They meet their destinies in the shallow gravels of the clear-water streams that run from the Alaska Range toward a distant Bering Sea. There are moose and caribou here among the boreal midlands and tundra uplands, but they are pruned and dispersed by limited forage, harsh winters, and roving wolves. Finding food requires carefully timed summer fishing and rugged winter work by skilled trackers. Human settlements have always been small. When I encountered the castaway, only about 150 Upper Kuskokwim Athabascans lived in the area's three villages, Nikolai, Takotna, and McGrath. Another five hundred or so non-Native in-migrants congregated primarily at McGrath. They are a hardy bunch.

In July of that year, we were traveling by skiff from Nikolai to the clear water of the Tonzona, a trip of about two hours. There were three of us in the flat-bottom riverboat enjoying a long, warm midsummer's day, a Nikolai friend deftly driving the boat, a Bethel friend, and me. As I say, ostensibly this was research. We were visiting traditional fishing sites of Upper Kuskokwim families.

Though this too is digression, I must tell you that the disappearance of the salmon fish traps on the Upper Kuskokwim was a sad event that could have been avoided. The fish traps of the Athabascan peoples of the Upper Kuskokwim were not grand affairs. They were small arrangements of V-shaped fences set during summer into the shallow river gravels to guide salmon into holding basket traps. The latticed construction was light, airy, and strong, allowing the free travel of water and fish. The trap was the epitome of good conservation, easily opened and closed to manage the passage of fish. They killed no unwanted fish. The fish were held alive for harvest or release. For hundreds, maybe thousands, of years the fences were opened and closed to provide sufficient escapement for spawning.

None of these traditional facts mattered to modern fisheries management. At Alaska statehood, a regulation was passed aimed at prohibiting the devastation of salmon by industrial-scale, commercial salmon fish traps elsewhere in Alaska. The blanket regulation was discovered to apply to the tiny subsistence salmon traps in places like Nikolai. Nikolai's salmon traps were probably the last to be used in Alaska. Sometime during the late 1960s, someone noticed the traditional traps around Nikolai and informed the village they were illegal. So the traps were dismantled under the blind eye of fisheries justice. For a little grace the ingenious indigenous traps might still be there. Of course, families must eat. So the Upper Kuskokwim Athabascans have continued catching salmon, shifting to hook-and-line attached to a rod-and-reel, with young boys casting and snagging fish in the same clear streams where the traps once were. Technically, rod-and-reel was sport gear, and sport fishing was legal. The dried salmon hanging in Nikolai's smokehouses attested to the toughness of traditional cultures. Age-old patterns were tenaciously persisting beneath a transformation of surface forms.

We were traveling to see an area where fish fences were once set. As we approached the fishing site, our friend driving the boat became increasingly nervous about the possibility of encountering the sequestered oddball who purportedly had taken up residence in a cabin nearby. Rumor had it that he was one of those no-good drifters who aimlessly travel roads until an end is reached. As too frequently occurs with drifters in Alaska, he had linked up with a poor local girl, herself adrift in Anchorage. With the girl he left the road system, flew to her village, and drifted farther yet by removing up to her grandfather's fish camp, pushed away from the village by fits of drunkenness and abuse. There he was abandoned, left by the girl after he broke her arm. At last report, he was still at the camp. If so, it would be hard to avoid him. Our outboard was loud in the quiet of the summer's day. Our route went directly past the camp. We were bound by traditional courtesies.

The signs were not good as we approached. There was a barking husky chained to a tree a half-dozen feet above our heads. There was smoke rising from a cabin tucked into the small trees. And there was the castaway. Waving and grinning on the riverbank like a grimacing Cheshire cat, and shouting like a carnival barker. "Come on up! The dog don't bite! She's friendly! There's coffee!" He looked like a gnome, completely shorn of hair, even eyebrows. His ears were jug handles set high on a sun-blistered head glistening slick with sweat. Defying the midday heat, he was unaccountably bulked up in a cotton plaid shirt, an overlarge denim jacket, and padded winter boots. Had he only one change of clothes? He grinned and grinned at us, wide, unblinking eyes flicking from one person to another as if searching for something familiar. He recognized Jeff, the boat driver. He couldn't place me, but his eyes lit up on seeing Elizabeth. He bellowed with the clarity of conviction, "Why, you're the gal from the post office at McGrath!" "No, I'm not," Elizabeth replied. Unfazed, rotating to Jeff, he broadly grinned and bellowed, "Well, don't she look just like the gal from the post office at McGrath!" "No, she doesn't," Jeff replied.

With a large, firm hand we were helped up the bank, then guided past the racks empty of fish or any signs of fishing. What was he doing here, if not fishing? We were ushered into the one-room cabin. It was not entirely a wreck; I have seen worse from single men. In the cast-iron stove a massive fire roared, a blast furnace in midsummer. The air was searing. He poured us cups of scalding coffee. In moments we three cordial guests were sweating as profusely as our host, grinning and agreeably nodding his head to news from town as if summer sauna sessions were normal. His wild eyes pleaded for talk. Talk, talk, talk about anything, he would listen, nod, and grin. Bits of dribble glinted in the slightly protruding and stretched lower lip, exudates from a wad of snoose packed beneath his gums. He deftly ducked to spit into a large coffee can sitting by the blazing stove on the cabin floor. In that surreal moment—my vision blurred in shimmering heat—I will always remember looking over to the coffee can. It was completely full and running over.

I should probably learn what happened to that tortured soul. I would guess he did not last in that cabin. Perhaps he survived at his girlfriend's village through the benevolence of its people. Perhaps he drifted elsewhere. They would know in Nikolai, as such events are remembered. The collective memory keeps track of the fate of those who drift away. In the castoff's face I could see the beginning transformations of unplanned solitude. The madness. It's true he may not have been entirely sound before the seclusion. Like the lost Yup'ik child who was retarded. Like most historical cases of so-called feral children, said to be tainted by factors other than what a researcher wants to assess. Natural experiments are real life, messy. But to me it makes sense that exceptional circumstances precede a sundering from the human community. Humans work hard to keep connected, to hold on to themselves and to others. Getting permanently removed takes a special person, unexpected events, or exceptional determination. The transformations of the lost usually are steps along much longer paths.

Because of the laws against transplants, I may never yet see transplanted elephants roaming an Alaskan steppe. Still, I think I have seen the northernmost lemon tree on earth, transplanted and growing in seclusion in an Alaskan sky. And also the northernmost coffee. I encountered them both in a remote homestead on the opposite side of the Denali massif, the more favorable eastern slope near Denali National Park. They were growing in a self-imposed isolation, testaments to the force of determination by a few humans to be self-sufficient and freed of humanity. I expect it's true that each ultimately bore witness to the unbearable costs of human liberation.

Denali National Park is among the most frequently visited Alaskan places. The area has been opened by rail, road, and small plane from the Nenana River drainage on its eastern edge. A resident of McKinley Park Village, near the park's headquarters, told me she moved here because it was the most magnificent place on Earth. Living in small cabins on homesites near the river, she and her neighbors serviced tourists during summer and ran dogs during winter. To her, this was the perfect life, nature's gift to a fortunate few.

"They're posy sniffers," was the derogatory assessment by one Healy resident just a few road miles to the north. Unlike McKinley Park Village, Healy was built on coal and power, a small community with strip miners working the valley's coal seams and electric-plant technicians generating power for Alaska's interior. Operating huge machines under physically harsh northern conditions, the hard hats' worldview might understandably differ from that of their McKinley Park neighbors who marketed ecosystems to tourists. "And they're food-stamp sourdoughs at Ferry," was a hard hat's hard assessment of the newcomers just to the north of Healy. In the area around Ferry, a historic river crossing, lived winners of homesites in a recent state-sponsored land disposal. Dozens of families were beginning the hard work of proving up their holdings, ten-acre lots interconnected by trails, physically divorced from jobs, amenities, and established communities. In this test of rugged individualism, federal food stamps to the homesteaders helped make ends meet.

A bit farther up the road was Anderson, at the time a small company town maintaining a solitary backscatter radar installation set on a ridge like an oversized drive-in theater screen, watching over the horizon for incoming nuclear missiles probably aimed at places like San Marcos. The radar workers received salary bonuses for accepting work assignments so far in the "tules," or "boondocks," they explained. This living-on-the-edge view might amuse the native Athabascans at Nenana village, a few more miles to the north, who lived near the center of their traditional homelands. Such was the cultural diversity of human settlements in the Nenana drainage, numbering about two thousand people all told when our research team conducted interviews in the area.

We were documenting fishing and hunting patterns in the newly settled drainage. We visited households in the potpourri of communities along the roads, "looking for subsistence users," according to those we interviewed. To help us look, they directed us along a branching network of referrals. We were encouraged to talk to trappers outside Ferry, mushers catching fish for dog food at McKinley Park Village, and big-game hunters with tracked, off-road monster-machines at Healy. But if we really want to find subsistence, we were told, we should not miss interviewing one particular couple. This man and woman lived a true subsistence lifestyle, they said, on their homestead up in the Nenana foothills. They had no phone. They were rarely in town. This time of year we could probably get there with a four-wheel-drive truck.

That winter's afternoon, I found myself nervously reading a scrawled sign on a makeshift gate, trying to decide how to proceed. It read something like, "Leave messages in the can," and was next to a dangling notepad and pencil. When temperatures dip past thirty degrees below zero on the Fahrenheit scale, I find it's hard writing messages on dangling outdoor notepads. I had just spent much of the afternoon negotiating a clunky four-by truck up narrow foothill tracks following directions supplied in town. The track followed a power line for a while. Leaving this, it followed a frozen dike pushed up from the musky earth. Up onto the valley wall it crept to this barrier, thrown across to block the path. Far ahead I could see low buildings, a sort of combined Quonset/trailer affair it looked, truck beds, cast-off motors, and other signs of human life. The message on the barricade continued something like this, "If you must go on, do so with much shouting and waving of arms." I could see no way to turn the truck around. So, leaving it behind, I continued on foot. I admit I did so nervously, with much shouting and waving of arms. I expected the bullet to come from the direction of the building, so I walked with an eye to the ditch. You may wonder how much this job paid.

I was met by a man holding a rifle. He was peering into my fur ruff for a familiar face. He was lean and tall, perhaps in his fifties. Despite the gun, when he spoke he displayed a gentle manner and a soft voice. "Oh, you didn't have to leave your truck back there," he apologized, as he opened his door to this unannounced stranger. The structure was warm and oddly shaped. Small rooms seemed to bud off in all directions from a larger, vault-roofed central chamber, the architectural fruit of years of labor. It was dimly lit from skylights. Reclining on a bed in one alcove was the woman of the homestead. Wan and long haired, she welcomed me with a demure smile and vaguely Continental air. She was rolling loose tobacco into cigarettes using some sort of hand-held device the size of a cheese grater, neatly stacking the finished products in a small wooden box, a task she continued throughout the interview. The quiet manners of the two partners intertwined like a self-supporting dance. I was placed in a comfortably soft chair, brought good coffee, and accorded rapt attention to every question. I sensed I was winter's first guest.

The formal subsistence survey went quickly. The man responded before the woman's backdrop of nods. Strangely, the answers were consistently no. Last year, did you take any salmon? No. Whitefish? No. Other freshwater fish, like trout or grayling? No. No fish at all? No. Moose? We used to, but not for a long time. Caribou? No, we used to, but not last year. Did you trap, like fox, beaver, lynx? Oh, no. And so on through the big game, small game, fur bearers, and birds. Porcupine caused a brief stir. Oh, yes, several porcupines. How many? Let's see, maybe five or six. Do you eat them, use the quills for crafts? Oh, no, no, we don't eat them, he explained, they get caught in the garden nets. What do you do with them? Feed them to dogs? Oh, no, I carry them off a little and let them go.

Putting down my pencil, I explained how I came to be there. I said, A friend of yours told me to come up here to find a true subsistence lifestyle. He looked surprised. "Who was that?" I named a trapper near Ferry. "Oh," he smiled in recognition, catching his partner's eye, "Yes. We haven't seen him for maybe two, three years?" "But you don't hunt," I asked? He laughed and said they hunted the four-legged Spam cans. Subsistence, that was something the Indians rightfully did, he thought, not them. But they did gather plants, the last items on the survey. Lots of berries—blueberries, raspberries, crowberries, salmonberries, cranberries. And a variety of other plants in season. They liked wild plants to augment their gardens. He took me outside for a short walking tour of the gardens, home plots for potatoes, cabbages, root crops, and herbs, now empty, cold, and hard in the low winter light. The porcupines were a problem, he said. They could be thwarted by nets strung high and loose. They fall backward when climbing and generally give up. They used to hunt but not anymore, from sympathy for the poor beasts. Now they didn't need to. They got some canned meat from town. How often did they visit town? A few times a year.

A sitting's too short for the presentation of a human life—reconstructed, recused, subplotted—so the barest outlines of paths were scratched out for me, the guest, leading to this retreat on the valley wall. He cared too much for people, he explained. In the Midwest, where he was born, a person could not even mow a yard without bothering someone, he said. He couldn't live that way. He searched in the North for places of greater freedom. They worked for a while in Healy. By chance, they acquired the homestead. The view was grand. From the ridge you could see Denali. A trailer park down below with walking trails to the ridge would bring in some money, but the state showed no interest in a road up this far.

Bit by bit, he and his partner settled in, built up the garden, improvised. He had earned a small pension of sorts, which, with the state's oil dividend check, was sufficient for what they needed in supplies, for the things they couldn't create themselves. The trips to town were fewer and fewer. They grew most everything they ate. His partner nodded, rolling and stacking cigarettes. Then he pointed above my head to a skylight. Looking up, I saw a dwarf tree suspended in a basket, hanging in the winter light with small fruits. "Are those lemons?" I asked, incredulous. They both laughed. "Over there are tomatoes," he said, pointing to another skylight. Even as he said it, I saw the tomatoes. "And over there is the coffee, but they don't do as well." I was stunned by the concept—coffee. Lemons, tomatoes, and coffee near the Arctic Circle, in the frigid Alaska interior, on the edge of Denali National Park. Sheer genius! Or, was it pure madness?

Great gulfs divide remote settlers beneath Denali and children lost on the tundra. Yet again, perhaps they are translations from a common text, accounts of wanderers who become lost, sundered from others, and searching for home. The icy winds whisper in the empty places—this way, this way—and wanderers follow. Set paths disappear. The channels become sunk under a featureless cold. The currents and tides grow stronger. It's not easy to find the way back.

Transformations come unbidden, autonomic, impelled. Visceral forces at work. They emerge like a stalking cat, hidden potentials released by harsh demands, as warm-blooded life has always responded, with speed and cunning, brush-lined holes, fur and full bellies, with ancient names like *aarayulit* or *ghwer-*. Old forms reclaimed. And if home is found once again, the transformed lost sing their rejoices in foreign voices, like a wolf's lament to a starry sky.

Or the transformations emerge through conscious self-reliance. These are frontier efforts at the edge of the social web constructed from self-will and self-involvement, worlds of one's own making, layer upon layer, a decoupage of self-applied culture. They produce surroundings fruitful and budding, dead and frozen, fenced against the solicitor's knock and a porcupine's hunger. They are personalized gardens transplanted to far-reached places. Autonomous. Freed. Nearly self-sufficient. If only the coffee would fruit, then no more coffee runs.

At Bethel it was too early for me to comprehend how the lost transform. What seemed easy for others to understand fell outside my experience, raised in a wealth of humanity. A child mutating in isolation was a hard story for me. No less hard after witnessing Sam the cat. Or the growing madness in the eyes of the abandoned on the Tonzona. Or even lemons swinging under skylights. But the North is a relentless teacher, and now I am beginning to get it, to personally feel it when I stop at traffic lights and fume, the meaning of too much humanity, and of too little. The empty places present dangers for the lost. Whether by self-willed choice or unhappy circumstance, most perish. Few can transform to survive. And if they do, what have they become? Is the lesson easiest to accept from a Yup'ik child, a feral cat, or a dead man's scrawl?

With the story of the reclusive coffee growers, there's a sad end report, one told by a failing hand. Just four years later the couple's self-imposed isolation found completion. That spring their bodies were found inside the makeshift home. The woman had died of natural causes in November. The man was dead a week later from a self-inflicted gunshot wound. After her death he had not sought help. Instead, he remained in the lap of solitude. He had lost all society, alone with himself and a partner's cold body laid out in an alcove. Beneath the desiccating watch from dimming skylights, he penned out the anguish, torment, and loss on a calendar, paper messages for some barrier firmly erected in life's path. Who can't imagine that last struggle, to continue ahead in complete solitude, or to turn back to humanity down the hill? I had stood at that very place myself, stood at that barrier in his path, looking both directions. At the time, I had worried about a gunshot coming from that solitary place. When it did, four years later, I was not surprised.

3

Respect

Bears and Humans, Flesh and Mind

It's best not to speak of bears. This wisdom comes from the Yup'iks of the Bering Sea. The Inupiat of the high Arctic teach this too, as do the Athabascans of the boreal forests. In your speech, use circumlocutions. Say *the dark one* or *the scary one* or *the smart one* and leave their names unsaid. People will know what you mean. When you hunt, hunt quietly, without fanfare or presumption, and with humility. For bears are powerful presences lurking on the edge of your thoughts, listening, and responding. This is the way with bears, for good or for bad. Equivocation is the most prudent course, because when we speak too much of bears, or even *think* too much about them, we tempt the unforeseen, the unintended. In the Far North I've learned there's this essential link, you see, between the bears in the flesh and the bears of the human mind. Each poses ancient dangers for the other. And you'll see that I've come to believe this is true not just for bears and humans of the Far North but for the bears in your mind too.

I remember my first encounters with grizzly bears—that is, with grizzlies in Alaska. I was standing inside the forest's edge just above the tide line on Admiralty Island. Kootznoowoo is its real, Tlingit name, "Fortress of the Bear," a vast island in the southeast archipelago swathed in great forests that mount up from the ocean toward snowcapped peaks awash in mists. I had been trolling for salmon with a friend when we beached the skiff to step ashore. The forest at tide line beckoned. So, climbing the short, steep beach, I stepped to its edge, an edge of light on the beach's side and of dark on the forest's. The view was astonishing.

I expected dense tangles of brush and trees like forests around my home in Juneau, messy regrowth from logging. Instead, I looked into old growth, a wide-open space capped by black-green canopies high above, vaulted roofs thrown out from girthy giants, spruce, hemlocks, and alder. Running beneath was silence. The forest floor presented no impenetrable clutter of brushy slash. It offered patchy glades of dim lights and shadows, dogwoods, forbs, and berries among decaying trunks nursing new saplings, with clustered boulders covered in moss like thick, undulating carpet. And everywhere ran trails, broad, meandering, and well laid, leading this way and that way, man-tall passages through the shrubs from glade to glade inviting the next step. My first naïve thought was, who maintains the trails? It was fleeting. My mind already was racing to rearrange signs into different sets of meanings. Stupid, I thought, north Admiralty Island has nobody, no *human* trail crews. And then I saw them, in my mind I saw them, the bears that made the trails, the huge bears, massive bears, hoary, grizzled bears slowly moving along the green, meandering paths set by a thousand passages. I saw them vividly, real and living, each and every one converging to greet me. And as I was completely unprepared for this meeting alone in their ancient fortress, without disturbing the silence I retreated back to the sunlit beach.

Soon after the dark bears of my mind became bears in the flesh, though not on North Admiralty and with others in retreat. It was near Brooks Camp in Katmai National Park, about eight hundred miles to the west toward the Aleutian Islands. I was watching, with the park superintendent, a small group of tourists fly-fishing chest deep in the crystal stream below Brooks Falls, surrounded by blood-red salmon. I had never before seen the contraptions each was wearing to keep upright and floating, a sort of full-body wader with blown-up inner tubes, from the center of which, suspended, the fishers cast with fly rods. "Rich Germans," the superintendent explained. Suddenly one near shore began to shout and wave, his excited warning just audible above the noisy river. He pointed toward the long, green grasses covering one side of the shore. We looked that way and saw the bear, a huge brown male, lumbering through the thick rushes that were parting like the sea before the hand of God. The bear paused on the bank, peering down on the salmon and the fishers. Three-quarter ton of wild life, waiting. The German fishers backed out of the water. Slowly descending, the bear replaced them. "We tell them here the bears have the right-of-way," the park superintendent whispered as we cautiously watched the bear fish mere meters from the Germans. "Each fish must be removed immediately for cleaning and locked storage at camp. This prevents associating humans with food. Everyone wears a bear bell. The grass is so high you can't see who's sharing the trail." "Sounds like a hassle," I said. "Oh, they love it," he replied. "It's part of the experience. So far, so good." And as if on cue, for no reason I could see, the bear finished fishing, rose from the river, and disappeared into the tall grass. The fly-fishers moved back in. The superintendent relaxed several notches. "That's Brooks Camp," he smiled at me with tired eyes, "an event waiting to happen." Humans and bears together, each poised for the next event.

In Alaska it's essential for children to learn about bears. It's a practical matter. Humans and bears run into each other. Encounters are not common. In fact, in most places meetings are rare and brief. People and bears work hard to avoid them. Even in Juneau, my late home, it was rare to meet a bear. This was so even though we lived as close neighbors, with bear densities among the highest in the world and rogues entering town for garbage every spring. Blue-ribbon committees struggled with garbage containment standards while SWAT teams firing rubber bullets chased bears in the wee hours. Bear relocation programs went over-budget, cruise ship tourists booked guaranteed viewings at Pack Creek, and hunters killed hundreds annually for food and hides. Yes, even when I personally saw several bears each year without looking for them, even so it was rare to actually meet a bear around Juneau. Except, of course, on the fringes of the mind—it was there that both you and your bears were very well aware of potential outcomes.

Children had to be prepared. My own two children received practical instructions in the Juneau public schools. Bears were a basic subject, like good touch/bad touch, fire safety, and drugs. Let's not mince words about the curriculum. It was folk knowledge, folklore pulled from the current local store, a human curriculum. Bears weren't guest lecturers. My children, Juneau's children, were given ideas about bears from teachers, parents, and friends. I expect it's generally true that bears constructed from these ideas now live inside our children's minds, internal guides for how to think and feel and act, prowling at the edge of light and dark.

My children learned there are two types of bears around Juneau—the great brown bears on nearby islands and the large-dog-sized black bears on the mainland, the ones seen around town. They learned to make noise when walking forest trails so as not to startle. They learned never, ever to run from a bear unless you want to be chased like a deer. Instead, talk directly to the bear in a nonthreatening tone and back off, carefully giving everybody ample room. If approached, wave your arms and make loud noises to say, "Hey, I'm a human!" They learned good mother bears protect their young, so watch out. Each bear has a personality, so expect surprises. If ever attacked, tightly curl into a ball and protect your face and play dead—if it's a brown bear. If it's a black bear, you fight back, hitting, kicking, and screaming. An attacking black bear is more likely to eat you, but most attacking brown bears aren't—they're roughing you up to leave you alone once you're small, inert, and nonthreatening. You hope.

How do you tell a black from a brown bear? "Climb a tree," explains my eleven-year-old. "If it climbs after you, it's black. If it knocks the tree down, it's brown. Ha ha ha," he laughs. He knows his bears. Having absorbed this local lore, my children are not only educated but also not a little bit unnerved by bears. By the bears in their minds. Because it's rare meeting the other kind, which is good.

There's an ancient lesson about bears meeting people, an instruction from the Tlingit and other northwest tribes. The whole account is properly told by clan heads, who rightfully hold it as heritage and property. But a sketch of the lesson has generally circulated. My daughter was taught it at school. It's represented on carved poles and in contemporary art. It's found at the museum. The lesson's been generously shared by the tradition bearers for the greater public good. As with most lessons, people come away with their own understandings. Here's the kernel of mine, abstracted from a larger whole better told by authorities other than me.

As I understand it, there are two young women gathering berries on a mountainside. Their family's boats are tied up far below them. While gathering, one woman sees the scat of a large animal and says something like, "Eeew!" Keep in mind, this is something my own children do while walking in forests. It's an almost involuntary reaction to the leavings of large animals. Yet this very human response is in fact a critical turning point in the story and presages all that follows. It is one of the lessons, as we come to see.

Later that day, as the two women head back toward the boats, the woman who exclaimed "Eeew!" spills her basket of berries. Hurry and catch up, urges her sister, leaving her behind to pick up the berries. Out of nowhere, a young man, a stranger, appears beside her. He's well dressed, well mannered, and, of course, very handsome. Without a word he helps the young woman reclaim the scattered berries. As occurs with matters of the heart, now the young woman faces a hard choice: to continue down the hill to her relatives waiting for her in the boats or to go with the stranger, who is headed up into the mountains. Of course she follows the handsome young man. I must say here that, not only have my children never done this, but my teen daughter scoffs at this part of the story, at the obvious foolishness of the young woman to follow a complete stranger simply because he's handsome, wealthy, and helped with her berries. But wait until she's older.

To make a longer story short, at his village she learns he's a headman's son. And she's in a difficult spot. She's hounded by his sisters. They mercilessly dog her heels to insult her, prepared to make the young woman's scats objects of derision. What goes around comes around. Yet the young woman transcends her difficulties. She prevails through cleverness. Burying her scats, she substitutes copper pieces broken from a hidden necklace. Oh! What a person of wealth! This ability, like the spinning of gold from straw, wins her the handsome young man in marriage. She gives birth to twin sons.

Later, the young woman's brothers return to search for their lost sister. Retracing her steps, they follow a game trail into the mountains. Without warning, a brown bear charges from the brush. The brothers kill it with spears. Their sister runs into view and falls crying upon the bear's body. "You've killed my husband," she weeps! Two cubs emerge from the brush. "These are my sons, your nephews. You must now care for them, raise them, train them, for I must stay." Bewildered at events, the brothers carry the two bawling cubs away in the boat. Nearing their home village, the cubs change bit by bit into human boys.

There are at least two practical lessons here for people. One is how to speak to a brown bear you meet. Since that time, because of that woman and her children, a kinship has been established between humans and brown bears. You may properly say, "Grandfather, I do not mean to bother you, I am simply looking for food, like you," and so forth. This is a show of respect. The other practical lesson is how to speak about scat or other signs of bears in the woods. You don't. Bears listen. This too is respect.

Single, alone, between marriages, blue, I was drinking one night in a Juneau bar. Guys drink at bars during blue periods hoping to meet someone who'll move them into a different color phase. A beautiful young woman, a stranger, appeared on the barstool beside me. She began to tell me a story. It was the truth, she insisted, and she could prove it. Though properly hers, I'll relate the tale as best I can from the sorry state I was in.

She was one of the perennially perky performers of the *Lady Lou Review*, a musical for tourists off the daily cruise ships. I'd seen it several times, an adaptation of Robert Service's "The Cremation of Sam McGee." Yeah, I know, the Klondike's in Yukon, not Alaska, and the end's a bit degrading for the high-kicking girls in red frilly shorts, but it's geared to please old tourists. Its performers are always fresh-looking talents just trying to earn some summer cash. It beats working slime lines.

She loved to hike, my bar mate admitted. So early one morning she packed Spam sandwiches, a banana, cookies, and juice and drove to the Sheep Creek trailhead, ten minutes from town. Now, this is an important point in the story, that she made Spam sandwiches. Everything turns on it.

Up the trail she went, through the coastal wood, up over the steep moraine, and down into little Sheep Creek Valley, a flat, quiet stream bordered by cottonwoods. It was there in the morning's solitude, strolling along the water's bank, that her world turned upside down. Suddenly and without warning, her skin pricked up. Cold dread spread along each arm. Jerking to a halt, sucking hard, mind churning, she wrestled with an intense, free-floating fear, peering this way and that among the stands of cottonwoods. Something was there. Then she choked, gasping for air, as a rank smell hit her full in the face. And then the thing emerged from the shadows, the bear, a large black bear, coming for her.

Forgetting every bear lesson, she screamed, spun, and bolted down the trail. In one second, wham! The bear flung her face down on the ground, riding her back. Groaning, breath punched from her lungs, she felt the world swirl as a great, foul-smelling weight pressed her into the earth. The sunlight faded. The last she remembered was—blechhh! Throwing up. She pantomimed at the bar.

She was puzzled when she began to come to. The ground pressed cold on her cheek. The flowing creek babbled. She cracked her eyes to misty light. She was still alive. She slowly lifted her chin from the mud, expecting to be crushed. Nothing. She eased her elbows beneath her. Nothing. She inched forward on hands and knees. Again, nothing. So she stood up and hobbled down the trail. Then she walked faster down the trail. Then she was skipping down the trail. Singing! All the way to the car, skipping and singing! It was at the car she noticed her backpack. The back of the pack was completely chewed off. Her lunch was gone.

"Wow," I said. "Wait, there's more," she replied.

She drove home. Showered. Dressed. And then she performed that afternoon on schedule in *Lady Lou*. Those young, perky actors have so much energy. Later, she felt stupid. The more she thought about it, the worse she felt. Taking up a pen, she wrote out the whole story like a confession for the newspaper so others might learn from her mistakes. For closure. Had I seen it? "Hmmm . . . no, I hadn't," I admitted. "But wait, that's not all," she said, touching my arm.

About two weeks later an odd package arrived, delivered to her post box. Inside the package was a greeting card addressed to her. Here are free gifts sent especially for her, it went. They wished her the best. Yours truly, signed, the Spam Company. The package held several cans of Spam, recipes for Spam, and best of all, a t-shirt with bold letters over a can proclaiming, *I love Spam!* "It's the truth," she said. "Here's the shirt!" And to prove it was true, lifting sweater to chin, she proudly displayed its scarlet letters for all in the bar to see.

Any branch of knowledge has its skeptics. Folk knowledge about bears is no exception. I know there are skeptics reading this right now who know they know bears better than Lady Lou, or the woman who married one. Perhaps they're right. We're all experts on the bears in our own minds. But I don't think anyone can rightly explain why that black bear didn't eat Lady Lou. She was passed out and helpless. Sure, she stunk like vomit, but bears eat pretty rotten stuff. He could have killed her, dragged the body up the mountain, and buried it like a deer carcass. Instead, he ate her sandwich. Black bears do kill and eat people, at least in Alaska. Alaska's chief epidemiologist statistically studied bear attacks reported in the papers during the recent century and found, much to the surprise of some bear experts, that while brown bear attacks were more frequent, attacking black bears were as likely to kill and eat the victim. Thus the local lore, lie down with browns, fight back with blacks. Polar bear attacks are the deadliest, though very rare because of where they live, on the ice packs. They're marine mammals eating seals and fish, but they'll actively stalk and kill humans given a chance. One smashed through a plate-glass window to eat a poor weather observer stationed on the Arctic slope a few years back, like smashing through the translucent ice above a seal den to extract a seal pup. But statistics can't explain this particular black bear. My teen daughter thinks people must taste pretty bad for a bear to prefer Spam. A Tlingit friend laughed and gave his explanation — "Why kill the golden goose, a good source of sandwiches?" But what can anyone say except that the black bear left her alive and free to go when it could have done otherwise.

The epidemiological study found that camping, fishing, and hunting increased the risk of attacks in Alaska. This geographic risk factor was linked with where bears lived, people placing themselves in harm's way. And the analysis uncovered another statistical surprise. Bears attacked non-Natives with greater frequency than Alaska Natives. Certainly biased news reporting was a factor in this, but this seemed short of a complete explanation. A behavioral factor was suggested. Could Alaska Natives be at less risk because of some special way they acted around bears? "Sure," replied a Yup'ik friend of mine, who thought he could guess the behavioral difference. "We carry guns."

In fall, two events hit Juneau's newspapers, brown bear attacks on hunters, one an Alaska Native, one not. The non-Native was hunting deer in the alpine meadows on Admiralty, the next island over from Juneau. In the early fall season, deer feed in the steep alpine toward the tops of mountains, and hunting's hard work. Later in the season, deer move progressively down the mountain slopes with the descending snowline. By December a number are found at sea level, feeding on kelp at the water's edge. The deer that jumps at the slightest sound in the alpine during October will stand stupefied on the beach during December, staring at a skiffload of hunters approaching by water. The genetic memories of predator threats encoded in deer brains do not yet include boats. My brain works the same with new technology.

In the alpine, the hunter killed a deer. He butchered it and stowed the parts he wanted on his pack frame. As he carried it down the mountain, a large male brown bear charged without warning from the brush. Before he knew what had happened, the bear whacked him into the willows, ripped off his pack, and dragged it a short distance away. Over the next half hour or so the bear defended the meat in the backpack, roaring and charging and whacking at the man sprawled in the muck. After a bit of this, the hunter was bleeding pretty good and falling into shock. He might have died except for the miracle of cellular phones, technology that has revolutionized hunting in Alaska. Weakly extracting one from his pocket, he dialed home and whispered his problem and GPS location. Within minutes, the Coast Guard was airborne. Like a scene from *Jurassic Park*, the chopper swept into the clearing, hauled aboard the blood-drained hunter, and raced him to the emergency room at Bartlett Hospital, where medics saved his life. The bear took off with the pack. When asked his take on events, the hunter said it happened so fast he couldn't do much. He figured he must have been reeking of deer blood, which might explain the bear's behavior. He profusely thanked everyone who saved him. The scars on his face wouldn't be too bad. Overall, he considered himself pretty darn lucky. That's good, eh? Lucky?

The second event played out on north Chichagof, the island next over from Admiralty, heading west. According to accounts, that afternoon an old Tlingit hunter left the village of Hoonah in his pickup truck, driving the uplands to hunt the logging roads. He was looking for deer in the new clear-cuts. Walking from his truck, he spotted and shot a deer. The shot was fatal, but the deer ran into a brushy patch to die. The hunter tracked it through thickets of small alders and willows to a clearing. The deer lay dead at its center. Just as he entered the clearing from one side, a large brown bear entered the clearing from the opposite. They both stopped, the human and the bear, eyeing the other, the deer between them. Well met. Now, that's luck, eh? Human and bear, each poised for the next event.

According to accounts, the old hunter addressed his unexpected company in Tlingit with an extemporaneous speech beginning something like the following. "Grandfather, this is the deer that I killed." To which the brown bear reportedly replied, "Roarrawl!" Or something like that. It was the hunter's turn to speak again. Respectfully and moving no major muscles, he further addressed the bear in Tlingit, saying something like, "My family will use this deer for food. We are a large family." To which the brown bear reportedly replied, "Roarrawl!" Or something like this, but even louder. The old hunter reported that the conversation continued in this fashion for some while.

Apprehending the course of negotiations, the old hunter finally addressed the bear in this manner. "I see that you have need of this deer too, so I will leave the deer that I killed for you." This said, the hunter slowly backed off through the edge of the clearing, away from the bear, carefully stepping backward. But stepping blindly, his foot caught a root, which tripped him up. Spinning around to break the fall, he turned his back to the clearing. Instantly the bear charged and whammed the man a fierce blow to the back. The force propelled him into the willows, landing him hard on his hands and knees. From this position he began worming his way through the thicket without turning. Crows appeared, flocking around him, calling out, flushed from their watching place. He stood up, staggering down the slope toward his truck. The crows circled wildly above, trying to tell him something, but he couldn't understand. He reached the truck and drove home, muddied and shaking from the shots of adrenaline. His wife insisted he immediately see the village health aide. So he did, checking out fine. He slept the night at home.

The next day, the old hunter returned with friends to the spot where he had parked the truck. He climbed the slope to retrieve the deer on the off-chance it might still be there. As he expected, it was gone. The bear had taken it. But on the trip up the slope, looking down on his tracks in the wet ground, he finally understood what the crows had been trying to tell him. On top of each of his footsteps was a large and deep bear print.

The Yup'iks of the Bering Sea mark the beginning of a person's life at the moment of awareness, when one's own memory begins. This starts about three or four with most children. Traditional public speeches don't begin with, "When I was born, . . ." but more commonly with the phrase, "When I became aware. . . ." Yup'ik infants certainly are alive, loved, and wondrously spoiled, but they are precursors of the persons they become, emerging into self-consciousness.

I remember my first bear encounter in California—like meeting the grizzlies in Alaska—a memorable event. I was walking a dirt road going nowhere in particular when I stopped to look at a moving trashcan with a hairy bottom. The bear's head came out of the can. He looked me in the eyes. Immediately, someone picked me up by my armpits, running. "That bear will not get you," I heard her shout. I felt very upset. She was *not* my mother. I was delivered into my own mother's arms at a campsite. I believe bears are my earliest memory, the moment I became me.

In taxonomic debates, don't believe those who say there are only two types of bears in North America—live ones and dead ones. That's just yahoo folk wisdom. There are at least three types—the bears in the flesh, the bears of the mind, and the bears in transition.

There were once thousands of grizzly bears in California, my newest home. Their conversion from bears in the flesh to products of the human mind was begun by the Spanish and perfected by the Yankees. The California rancheros roped them from horses. With less cultural flair, the California Yankees just shot them by the score. The last record of a dead grizzly in California was in 1922. I understand that there are even now a number of black bears, particularly near places like Sequoia and Yosemite. Their conversion is still being perfected.

True and original conservationists, Californians hold fast to the idea of grizzly bears. They like it and haven't let go. The grizzly bear strides toward a lone star on the state's flag. The grizzly bear growls beside Minerva's feet on the state's seal. The California grizzly is accorded the highest honor as the official state animal, in spirit if not in flesh. The curious can still view facsimiles in zoos, imported from Alaska or Montana, if they're awake and pacing in their exhibits. But they're not California grizzlies. These can never be caged or bred by some zoological society. The real California grizzly bear has been freed of the flesh. It lives free as an idea, deliberatively revived by the people's representatives in 1953 and legally propagated as the official symbol of the Great State of California, the Bear Republic, striding and growling on every flagpole and state podium. We won't have it otherwise.

Our family met with California bears shortly before making our move to the Golden State. We were camping our way north through the Gold Country following California Highway 49, named for the 49ers whose gold fever instantly transformed California from a territory wrested from Mexico in 1848 to a full-fledged state in 1850. California Yankees don't waste time. Climbing into the Sierra foothills, we were set up to camp on the outskirts of Sequoia National Park at a small canyon site called Buckeye Flats, for the buckeye trees there, about three thousand feet elevation, not quite into the pines or redwoods.

We had just finished placing our tent when a neighboring camper shouted out something about bears, instantly energizing all around us. Coming up the bottom of the steep-sided canyon in which the campground was set was a mother black bear with a cub. To me, she looked somewhat smaller and thinner than the Juneau versions. In the building excitement a pale-green truck with an official logo pulled up, disgorging a young woman dressed in that odd green hat and matching blouse and pants that forest officials are forced to wear. She began to shout instructions at the campers, issuing orders to everyone as the two bears scrambled up the steep scree above our heads. It was plain to see that the easy way up the canyon was blocked by tent sites and motor vehicles. The bears were taking a less-easy route, perhaps to avoid the campers. Partway along, the mother bear stopped and looked down at the flurry of activity just below her.

The green woman rushed a few steps up the slope directly at the bear, arms waving above her head, yelling, "Yaaaah! Yaaaah! Go away bears! Yaaaah!" The mother bear stood unmoved, watching with head going side to side. The cub was hidden somewhere in the brush beyond her. "Yaaaah!" yelled the green woman again, picking up a handy stone and chucking it at the bear. Turning to the crowd, she yelled instructions to the campers to form a line, shoulder to shoulder, men, women, youths, children. Shoulder to shoulder they all lined up, eager to be recruited. Unfamiliar with this tactic, probably because they were uninformed Alaskans, my daughter and son did not rush to join the human chain. Neither did I. But we saw what was coming. Following their mother's nod, my children cautiously slipped into the car and shut the door.

"Yaaaah! Yaaaah! Go away bears!" shouted the green woman, lunging forward with the line of humans at her back. It was not a pretty maneuver compared with, say, a halftime marching band or an English battalion stiffly plunging into withering fire, but, to be fair, these have practiced. As a ragged unit, campers chased up the hill behind the green woman shouting their own yaaaah-yaaaahs and heaving their own sticks and stones. Suddenly the mother bear moved, but unexpectedly she moved downward, toward some of the rushing campers. Not a charge, but just moved downward. This momentarily created disarray as young and old campers scattered, though others persisted at the edges. Then she seemed to hesitate, went right and went left, scattering people, and finally turned around and moved higher up the slope into the brush. A little flash of black showed the cub had followed. On the ground, the campers were buzzing with self-congratulations and personal accounts of their roles in the fray. My preteen daughter opened the car door and asked me, absolutely puzzled, "*What* are they *doing?*" Perfecting human-bear relations in the California parklands.

That evening I conferred with the green woman's boss, a slightly older woman carrying a wider and more cluttered belt. I was seeking information and asking questions. She never smiled once. Unlike the superintendent at Katmai years before, there was not even a hint of laconic pleasure in the tired eyes about bear-camper encounters. No, this was a hard institutional look of a camp under siege. And not just from bears. "We must train the bears," she was explaining to me, "to be averse to humans, to overcome the attraction to food." "Wasn't it risky," I offered, "recruiting children to run at a mother with a cub and the leader without even a gun?" The *gun* word jerked her upright. "The employee's class doesn't allow for a gun," she tersely replied. "But she didn't even have a can of pepper spray," I offered, "if the mother had attacked a child." "The bear would not have attacked," she replied with certainty. "How could one know," I responded, "with bears as they are?" "It would not attack," she replied with finality. And the conversation ended.

The siege commenced later that night with the dousing of the last campfires. Shouts and shrieks. Flashing lights. Banged pots. Siren blasts. The mother bear and cub had returned, perhaps, or some others. We listened from our sleeping bags. In the morning, we surveyed the general damage around camp. Junk strewn about several of the campsites. Clotheslines down. A cooler box crushed. "But," we were told by knowing campers, "it's much worse up the road at Lodgepole Camp, inside the park. There each night car doors are pried off for anything resembling a food cooler," they said.

So on our first night camping near Sequoia we began to learn of a different folk knowledge current among Californians. With the public, the experts wielded a collective knowledge of a different sort. Theirs was a familiarity with bears that differed from the respect taught by Yup'iks, Inupiat, and Athabascans. It dealt with yaaaah-yaaaahing and battle lines and rock throwing and lockboxes. It was taught where humans were packed into campsites along streambeds traveled by bears, near reserves of land inside ever-shrinking open spaces. And it dredged up for me another old adage in the folklore concerning a kind of familiarity. The adage about familiarity breeding contempt. And how maybe it was just as true for bears as for people. We skipped Lodgepole Camp.

At the annual Alaska Folk Festival in Juneau, two of our more successful songs have dealt with bears. Along with political gibes, Juneau crowds love bear songs. We sang one about cleaning up garbage to the tune of "Ghost Riders in the Sky," with original lyrics that in part went like this: "Some bears are smaaaart, some bears are daaaah-umb, keep gar-bage bears on the raaaah-un!" Applause! Yeah! Keep garbage bears on the run! The other we sang, "Waltzing with Bears," originally a Dr. Seuss song, features Uncle Walter sneaking off day and night to go wa-wa-wa-waltzing with bears, a popular refrain resoundingly joined by the festival crowd. Yeah, waltzing with bears! What's not generally known, however, was that, before the folk festival that year, the head of Juneau's blue-ribbon bear committee had called the head of our singing group, the author of the garbage bear song, in an effort to achieve, if not exactly censorship, at least some artistic self-restraint. The bear committee head said he was personally uncomfortable with the term "garbage bear" and its connotations for the people of Juneau. He was asking the singing group to reconsider using those words in the song. He preferred a newer, less pejorative term than "garbage bear" for Juneau's annual bear invasion. What was that, the songwriter asked? "Urban bear."

The conversion of bears in the flesh to products of the mind is a widespread endeavor. It occurs not just in California but in cosmopolitan Juneau, where the half-dozen garbage bears shot annually produce blue-ribbon bear commit-tees whose members test the waters of folk taxonomies, as if wild bears eating human garbage were a lexical problem solvable through a careful word con-struction grabbing at other parts of the human mind. Like the humble Alaska Tanner crab known as "opi crab," whose sales lagged until receiving a little lexi-cal assistance, getting christened the Alaska "snow crab." Sales soared. Another victory of mind over matter.

As part of this evolving urban mythology, one spring in Juneau a mother bear emerged from her den with a special cub. The cub was a so-called glacier bear, a category in the local folk taxonomy for a black bear with a pale blue coat, like the color of recently fractured glacial ice. In the newspaper, experts explained that glacier bears were simply an uncommon color phase found in local black bear populations, not a separate race or subspecies, despite contrary claims. Glacier bear. It tugs at the mind.

Juneau seemed enchanted by the baby blue cub. In the following weeks the mother and cub frequented the slide path on the slope of Mount Juneau right above town. With binoculars people stood in town and watched the special bear chase its mother, who was feeding on new shoots. The paper published the celebrity's picture. During lunch, downtown workers strolled a few minutes up Gold Creek to catch closer views, momentarily forgetting the goofball state politics in the legislative chambers. It was a sunny, spectacular spring, fresh and pure, like the little glacier bear romping on the mountain slope.

Then the mother and cub disappeared. The experts said they had moved higher up with the melting snows to forage farther from people, as smart bears do. Soon after, the annual spring invasion of town began. Bears not wise enough to go up came down. Trashcans were raided. Dogs terrorized. Bears trapped, tagged, and relocated. The public self-examination resumed on municipal trash standards and bear policies. It was a more-or-less routine spring for Juneau, a town blessed to be near wild lands supporting large and healthy bear popu-lations.

Then came an unhappy report. The glacier bear was spotted, not high in the wilds but down in the dumps. Mom had come to town. The cub was learning the city life. Many were anguished, knowing the fates of garbage bears habitu-ated to humans and human trash, unable or unwilling to reform. Trapped and relocated, some were killed by dominant bears in unfamiliar territory. Others found their way back for recapture and destruction. Then came the news, the glacier bear had indeed been trapped by Fish and Game. Phones rang off the hook with advice, support, and threats. What should be done with this misguided waif caught red-handed but still true blue in the collective mind? Calls were made. Arms twisted. Muscles flexed. The Anchorage zoo expressed a willingness to accept a glacier bear. An airline offered free passage. State workers volunteered. A plan fell into place. So it was that, with mixed emotions, Juneau bid adieu to its little blue friend, who flew off to a life in a cage, which might be better than no life at all, or might be worse.

That would have been that for the blue bear tale were it not for a muckraking follow-up published from Anchorage. Scandal at the zoo! The rare glacier bear was seen lying depressed in a small enclosure. The tiny cub seemed lethargic, malnourished, sick, at least to the reporter. How could this happen? "We're just a small zoo," was the reply, "doing the best we can for him." So outraged was the Alaska public that the zoo enjoyed its best attendance ever. Anchorage residents who had never even known that they had a zoo flocked in droves to see for themselves the poor glacier bear. Donations poured in with visitor receipts. "Save the glacier bear!" Who suddenly revived. It seemed as if goodwill and good health were linked. A new and larger exhibit space was built with the generous donations, as chronicled in the paper. And so the glacier bear, now named Taku, lived, happily ever after. The transitions were complete, from black to blue, from garbage to kennel rations, from a wild bear to a named urban bear, from a bear in the flesh to a bear of the collective mind. Maybe he'll be bronzed.

For humans it's best not to speak of bears, or even to think too much about them. As I age, this wisdom grows clearer for me, observations from the Yup'iks, the Inupiat, and the Athabascans. And I suspect the Tlingits have it right too. Bears and humans do share a distant kinship from that woman who spoke without thinking. They are like uncles from a collateral side that branched off long ago, or great-great-grandfathers removed by a vast span of years. It's a great distance that commands the greatest respect, a relationship demanding mutual acknowledgment and the most cautious formality when bridged. It's a distance that should be preserved.

That humans and bears can somehow learn to live together in camps or towns is folklore of another sort, a teaching sadly misguided and ultimately destructive. Open lands and human settlements cannot be conjoined into some Ursinotopia where humans stroke the backs of great shaggy beasts, peaceable kingdoms where lions lie down with lambs. I've seen that, for short times and in specific places, the two great families can tolerate each other's presence. Fly-fishers observing a careful right-of-way, moving aside when Grandfather fishes. Camera buffs on designated hillocks snapping images of annual bear convocations. Or cubs watching from high slide paths the legislative aides watching back. But increasingly I'm unconvinced of the possibility of an urban bear, except for those images of bears I've seen surrounded by moats in exhibits pacing back and forth, back and forth, back and forth. And I cannot imagine hungry bears learning respect from campers throwing stones and shouting yaaaah-yaaaahs and squirreling away food inside lockboxes. The bears of my mind are not these captured or bamboozled products. They loom large, dangerous, and free, powerful beings whose distant kinship I'm glad to acknowledge, and at a respectful distance.

I've seen what transpires when humans speak glibly of bears and consciously seek them out, driven like Uncle Walter for whatever reasons to go waltzing. Stop us, please. The bears of the flesh will respond. They do dance with us and are destroyed in the clutch. They start as bears in the flesh and then transition into bearlike things, products of human ingenuity, freed of the open places where flesh bleeds and bodies die and someone eats: bears rummaging through garbage dumps, grizzlies growling from flagpoles, bears singing on celluloid and dancing in mechanical cabarets, unable or unwilling to break loose or climb down to follow the melting snows, glorified or despised but rarely respected.

My children are more than a bit unnerved by bears. I am too. For this I'm glad. The bears within our minds serve to hold us at a respectful distance. My children and I have learned to be wary of bears in the flesh, to believe in their great power, unpredictability, and heightened sensitivities to what we say and intend and do. The bears of our minds roam as great beasts, still free, setting trails in the open places that bears and humans sometimes share, places that should be kept open, undisturbed. And with my unease, I'm content to walk the paths of their island fortresses, anticipating those rare times during passages when we both may meet in the flesh, bears and humans together, face to face and eye to eye. Oldest memories. Ancient and dangerous kindred. Poised for the next event.

4  Grace

Peace of Mind and Chaotic Systems

There are spiderwebs as big as dinner plates hanging between trees in our new California home. We see them, my daughter and I, on foggy mornings walking to the bus stop. She misses these early morning mists that gather down her long hairs and drip beneath her collar. The mists were everywhere in the rainforests of the North Pacific where we once lived. They remind her of home. In our new home we enjoy the mists only on exceptional cool mornings with the right dew points. But California orb spiders must hate them. The fogs create havoc with their remarkable webs, those cleverly constructed concentric circles hung aloft on anchoring threads. We have seen what happens as the mists settle. The invisible orbs gradually appear, materializing between the trees as dangling strings of pearls in the morning light. What flying bug could fail to notice? And sometimes the insubstantial mists augment the tiny pearls with water, molecule by molecule, growing larger until, heavily weighted, a key strand breaks, collapsing the web into itself. Ah, the poor spider. The creature must start over, pulling in the wet strands, consuming them, and reconstructing the web again from the ground up, all because of floating mist and a single broken thread.

I was born in California, I think, because of a single broken thread. A small death. It was an insubstantial event in the overall pattern of things, yet all-important to me, for I would not be alive. It was a broken strand that caused a temporary collapse and reconstruction. I know little about it except as a family footnote. My paternal grandmother's third baby, a girl, was stillborn. How or why, I don't know. But they say my grandmother was consumed by grief. So they sent her away from the pain of her West Virginia home to relatives in Southern California. And that's how it happened. My grandfather and two young boys, one my father, joined her. A generation later I was born a Californian instead of not being born at all.

On one of the morning walks my daughter asked about weather and butterfly wings. Was it really possible that a butterfly might cause weather in California by flapping its wings in Tibet? I don't know. But I think I understand the parable. There's an ultimate unpredictability in natural systems like weather such that small changes in initial conditions can have profound outcomes. The butterfly effect, attributed to MIT meteorologist Edward Lorenz, is the idea that the mere flapping of a seagull's wings (eventually, butterfly wings in Brazil) might determine the fate of life a hemisphere away (a tornado in Texas). Such natural systems are said to have histories and futures defying logic and security, except the logic of chaotic systems and the short-term assurances of meteorologists employed by the evening news. In their most frightening aspects they are realms where, periodically and unforeseen, asteroids descend from the sky, wiping clean the slate and resetting the clocks. Where tiny molecules condense to collapse life's fabric. Where the unaccountable deaths of unborn babies drag the human heart into deep despair. Such are the natural systems that wrench from despairing humans a cry for grace. And force spiders to incessantly rebuild.

Living on the edge in the Far North has given me an appreciation for the random event, the serendipitous, the chaotic. With butterfly wings in mind, how do you understand this northern event? It happened near my house in Bethel. Is it an inexplicable series of accidents one frozen winter night? Or, was it grace?

To help give it a proper assessment, first understand the flow of booze. At the time I lived there, Bethel was a *damp* community, neither *wet* nor *dry*. *Damp* was a legal condition created by its good citizens. A majority plainly saw the human devastation created by the sale of alcohol in wet communities, yet couldn't bring themselves to ban alcohol completely as a dry community. So the voters split the baby. They allowed imbibing alcohol if purchased elsewhere — flown or barged in from points south — but prohibited buying and selling. Under this contorted legal compromise between personal freedom and public health, local bootleggers did a brisk business.

Like humanity most everywhere, there were alcoholics in Bethel. One poor woman in particular I noticed around town, chronically drunk by midday, wandering from place to place. She was short and stocky in her parka with a broad smile of missing teeth. She peered into faces in a consistent search for something good. The inexplicable series of accidents involved her. Events must be reconstructed in part, as she didn't remember. But apparently late one afternoon in the winter's dark the poor woman passed out from too much drink on the side of an icy berm near the Catholic church. She slipped from sight to a frozen pond below. It's a bad place to be sprawled unconscious, in the blackness, on the hard ground, far from human concourse, with night temperatures dipping below zero.

Sometime that night a taxi was called. Surprisingly, tiny Bethel, a place with five thousand people, hosted a fleet of taxicabs. For a couple of bucks a beat-up cab would pick up people in minutes and transport them anywhere in town, to a friend's house or the store or the armory's bingo, wherever, saving a hard walk on slippery ice in stiff winds off the tundra. It's a wonder the low fares could keep so many cabs running in such a small town.

On this night the cabbie picked up riders in one subdivision to take them to another. To shave a few minutes from the ride, the cabbie took a shortcut across one of the frozen lakes in town. Bethel is built on tundra, a flat alluvium pockmarked by ponds. Frozen in winter, the sloughs and lakes are used as highways by snowmachines, four-wheelers, dog sleds, and, more occasionally, by taxicabs. That night the cabbie drove down a short bank onto the lake, cruised across the smooth ice, and drove up the opposite bank into the adjoining subdivision. It was on the gravel road that they all heard and felt something funny with the cab, like a flat tire or dragging muffler. So he stopped. Checking the tires and muffler, the cabbie was surprised to find a body beneath the cab. Police and paramedics with blinking red lights swarmed around the vehicle, jacking it up to remove the body. The riders hailed another taxi.

Extracted, the body turned out to be a woman, still alive but unconscious. She was rushed to the hospital. Not only was she alive but she was uninjured, unconscious not from injuries but from booze. It appeared that the cab, picking its way down the bank of the frozen lake in the blackness, drove over the woman lying on the berm, straddling her with its tires. She was caught in the undercarriage and dragged under the car across the lake and up onto the gravel road on the opposite bank. Moreover, because of her prone position, bulky parka, and icy surfaces, she was effectively cushioned the whole journey. The driver stopped in time to avoid much injury, alerted by the friction from the graveled surface. She awoke in the hospital unaware of what had happened—a bit bruised and scratched, but that was all. Further, the doctors believed this saved her life. Had this not happened, she would have frozen to death lying unnoticed in the dark.

The imperiled accept salvation in most any form. Yet there's a particular symmetry to this rescue of a poor chronic drunk saved by a taxicab. The main bootleggers in town were the taxicab drivers.

Perhaps it's needless to wonder overly much about events like this, but how do you understand it? This was merely a series of accidents, correct? There are other poor souls who do perish, undiscovered. Still, being unwittingly saved in the blind dark by a differential gear seems a peculiar salvation to me. The probabilities are astonishing if you begin to think about them — if she had passed out elsewhere, if the cabbie had taken the road, if the car had descended over to the left, if the undercarriage had been three inches lower, if the ice had been less smooth. These were the small details, each of which mattered, that fell into place. That was the sheer luck of it, the amazing chance coordination. The probabilities were infinitesimally small, but everything clicked. It's just the human mind that imposes deeper patterns and meanings on what is at root pure chance or coincidence within chaotic systems, right?

But in the event's postmortem I heard it said several times. It was not her time. *Not her time*. Think on this awhile. Like chaos itself, this too is a wonder. Imagine all that *it* implies. *Not her time*. For the rational human mind, this other perspective may pose greater difficulties than convictions in randomness. It becomes a question of grace.

There's a story told of how tribes of the Southwest came to live at the center of the world. The Water Spider found it. Spider stretched out his legs in all directions and found he could not touch the West. So the people moved west. He stretched again and touched west but could not touch south. So they moved south. And so it went until he stretched out his six legs and could touch the edges of the world in all directions. And that is where they settled, at the very center.

I stood near the center of the world on Black Mesa in northern Arizona toward the end of the turbulent sixties. For the college-aged like me this was a period of turmoil, counterculture protests, and new political activisms in the United States. We were sucked up by historic events. One afternoon three of us, UCLA undergraduates, threw sleeping bags and highway maps into a car and took off for northern Arizona. It was one of those spur-of-the-moment impulses.

We had been seeing political placards around campus decrying the desecration of the sacred lands of the Hopi and Navajo nations by strip-mining on Black Mesa—"digging up the bones of Mother Earth." We wanted to see for ourselves. Why not? There were roads and maps.

So there we stood on Black Mesa, three long-haired, blue-jeaned punks facing a hard-hat foreman of the Peabody Coal Company beside a dusty trailer on the edge of a growing strip-mining operation, about as far from town as a person could be but fairly near the Earth's center. The foreman was trying to decide what to do with us, whether to boot us off or shove us into one of the reclamation trenches. Instead, he threw us into his truck and gave us a personal tour. He showed us the monster machines ripping off tons of overburden and scraping out the great seams of coal that would be pounded or mixed into fine slurry for conveyance by train or through pipes to the coal-burning electrical generating stations near Lake Powell and in southern Nevada. The massive scale of the operation was overwhelming. It still stays with me. Trench walls towered like skyscrapers. Thick, black veins ran for miles in all directions. Colossal loads were wheeled on giant tires that could squash men like bugs. The scale is what I remember. Compared to the hugeness of the mesa and the coal seams and the blasted rock and the machines, the actual workers were specks, tiny afterthoughts flitting among the canyons and rubble, employed to engage the levers in a giant circumstance unfolding itself at the center of Mother Earth. And this is what I discerned from all I saw—we were three more specks.

It was near here that my own life's thread was inexplicably left uncut. The event took place only a handful of years after the Black Mesa visit, though even now this seems to me to have been several lifetimes later. I was married. I had a new daughter. And I had a job prospect. My new father-in-law had offered me summer work. It was an opportunity to earn some money between semesters. As will be in a world of coincidence, I had married the daughter of the site superintendent charged with overseeing the construction of the coal-fired electrical generating station at Lake Powell. I would be building the very station feeding from the Black Mesa mines I had toured scant years before. Pure random chance. I was conflicted by prospects, particularly by the environmental and cultural implications of building electrical generating stations on Navajo land. "Hell," my father-in-law snorted, "the plants were overengineered for pollution." They were designed with scrubbers and precipitators and self-regulators. The emissions would be hardly more than steam. It was in the contracts. There were apprentice programs for Navajos and Hopis to help build and operate the plants. It was good employment. And, poor college students getting paid a decent wage should learn to deal with conflict.

I had been driving all night from Los Angeles, scheduled to arrive in northern Arizona sometime the next day. Riding with me was my wife, asleep, and our baby tucked in an infant seat, with piles of junk for a summer's stay. In the black of night the desert highway was quiet, monotonous, hypnotic. I pulled over to sleep. We were stopped on the edge of Utah and Arizona on the open, red-rimmed plateaus approaching the center of the world, just moments from death.

The rising sun woke me, crunched in the front seat. With a sip of coffee, I pulled out on the highway for the last leg. I must have driven less than a thousand heartbeats when I reawoke at the wheel, hurling through sagebrush at a great speed. I had fallen asleep. The car had left the road and I was no longer in control. I could apprehend nothing other than the sensation of high speed and the blur of sagebrush scraping by the windows and then a soundless soaring through the air. It was at that moment, that time nearest death, when I heard a voice within me, a clear voice, simply saying, "It will be all right." And I understood this to mean, it—everything that was about to happen—it will be all right.

The car crashed. It had jumped a ravine according to the troopers examining where the tracks had left one side and appeared on the other. The suspension shattered with the force of the landing. The front wheels broke and cramped to the side. The car dug into the ground broadside, dragging to a stop. And then silence, except for a tiny wail of a baby. We searched among the piles of junk because the infant seat was empty. We found her, like we found ourselves, unhurt. The car was a wreck. But we were unhurt, surrounded by a vast land of red mesas and canyons and rocks beneath a vast pink sky brightening with a new day, standing alone and inexplicably alive near the center of the world. It was not our time.

It was in the northern Arizona desert that a natural explosion shut down the power plant. I sat up on the steel about 165 feet above ground when the first tiny bugs appeared. Ping. Ping. They flew into the lights. This began during the second shift, about ten at night. Powerful lamps illuminated the job site. The bugs came in from the surrounding blackness. Ping. Ping. Ping. It increased with frequency. I picked one up to examine it, a green, box-shaped creature about the size of popcorn killed from the collision or the heat of the light. I had never seen one before. Ping. Ping. Ping. Ping. Ping. The collisions increased in intensity and volume, like a coming hailstorm. Looking up, I saw what looked like the night's darkness drifting into the lights, sweeping like shadowy curtains blowing in thicker and blacker, swarms of green, box-shaped creatures drawn in from the desert, drawn by the flood lamps. They hit and died by the thousands, by the hundreds of thousands, mounding up on the ground beneath every light. The air became choked with flying boxes. The air stank with their burning bodies. Lights began to shatter. Compressors shut down. Motors whined to a halt. Men scurried for cover, hunkering down beneath the green torrent. For a half hour at least, I would guess, I watched from my scaffold perch a world overrun. Then it was over, as quickly as it had begun. The air cleared and hushed. All that remained were mounds of green carapaces. It happened only once.

I saw the first death about the second week, a Navajo apprentice to the carpenters' union, I think. He carried a load and walked into a hole, falling a great distance. The hole appeared at the foot of a stair about a hundred feet up. An electrician working on something there had not replaced the grating. With his arms full, not watching his feet, the apprentice stepped into it, where there should have been grating, where there had been grating just minutes before. "It happens," they told me. And then would come stories about Joe and Red and other poor saps who had died because of a rope or a bolt or a mistake. At the quitting time whistle I watched the first shift shinny down the steel and run for their trucks. Three abreast on the two-lane highway the trucks raced toward the bars to get in those drinks before heading for home. Strong men coping with strain.

"Don't take anyone drunk up on the steel," they ordered me. I was hired to operate the basket lift. "No one's supposed to drink but some do," they said. "If they're drunk, sit still no matter who threatens you." When I first came on the job they asked, who you kin to? I wasn't known and had not come off the union bench. Who you kin to? Then they pulled from the shelf an amber, labelless bottle and offered me a drink, a dare for a hundred dollars, with snickers all around. A worker sucking out the porta-potties had found it, jamming up the suction pump. Some slob in the can had shoved it between his legs to get rid of it. Look, the cap was tight, it was still good.

I first heard of oil money sitting in that trailer from a teamster. Jobs were drying up in Arizona, he said. The real money was the oil pipeline in Alaska. That's where he was headed. Screw this desert heat. He was quitting tomorrow and heading north. I remember at the time that it seemed an odd way to live, running from job to job, from state to state. Where's the security? Ten years later I myself would be scraping together a life in Alaska researching subsistence, mandated by a law from a federal lands act created by the trans-Alaska pipeline, earning money from oil, making a living from chaos and grace.

When I first came to Alaska, I was surprised to find a convention common in some Alaska Native villages—the last person to leave a house tied the house door shut with a string. There was a stout nail pounded into the outer door-frame protruding a few inches. The last person wound a light string several times around the nail, attaching it to the door. "Why was this done?" I asked. For wind pushing open the door and dogs getting into the entryway, they explained. Also, the string shows visitors that no one's home so they don't waste time knocking or entering. The string announces this house is momentarily unoccupied. I have come to learn in these village homes that security is found not in locks but in neighbors.

In our Juneau home we did not lock doors. In Juneau locks froze shut in the snow and thaw cycles, especially car doors. Car door locks were more trouble than benefit. There was a car thief who periodically rifled through the cars on our block looking for spare change, leaving the glove compartment open and the ashtray pulled out. I suppose we sometimes had some to be found. This was much better than frozen car door locks. We also left our house unlocked but not because of frozen latches. This was sometimes very hard to do, particularly hardest one week after an unsolved rape in town. I explained to my daughter and son why we did it. We left the house unlocked in case strangers ever needed to get in, particularly drunks. Probably this would never happen. But in a chaotic world you couldn't predict, it might happen some night. So to be safe, we kept the doors unlocked.

I observed my first tragedy with doors my first year at Bethel. I learned the cruelty of the false security of doors in a world of chaos and random events. A party was going on in one of the trailer courts, just on the road toward the airport near the Fish and Wildlife Refuge housing. A young Yup'ik man left the party to pee in the willows. Coming back in the dark one trailer must have looked like another to him. He'd been drinking and wasn't from town. So by accident he reentered the wrong trailer. He did not knock, and the door opened. The trailer's owner said he was frightened awake by someone coming through the front door he thought was locked. He grabbed a pistol next to his bed and shouted a warning. As the intruder continued to come, he shot in the dark, killing the man.

They did not charge the killer, to the outrage of many. On the Yukon-Kuskokwim Delta people did not shoot at visitors who did not knock before entering unlocked doors. In the villages, houses usually had two doors, an outer door to an Arctic entryway and an inner door to a living area. The outer door was commonly unlocked. You knocked at the inner door, if at all. But the killer was not from the delta. He came from one of those other places where security is promised by doors you thought locked against strangers, and if not, by loaded guns on bed stands. In those places, it seems, this kind of thing was permissible.

The second freak event did it for me completely, the accident in Fairbanks several years later. A young Inupiat woman from northwest Alaska visited her aunt in the city. They both went to bingo. The aunt came home early while the niece lingered at the nearby bars to socialize and to drink. She walked back to the neighborhood later that night, probably drunk and confused, for she never found the way to her aunt's home. From interviews the police learned neighbors heard sounds like a drunk calling in the dark. No one responded. They found the young woman the next morning, curled up by a backdoor stoop a few doors down from her auntie, frozen to death. The door she was by was locked.

I tell this story to my children. How small events can lead to tragedies like these. We kept our doors open just in case. At least a person like this young woman would be able to find her way in to a place of warmth. We might find her lying on the floor in the morning, cold, embarrassed, and alive. A victim of bad choices and unlucky circumstance, spared by a little grace.

In our morning walks, my daughter and I pass other round things floating above the grass that are not spiderwebs. They are home security signs poked into the lawns of every fifth house or so. Some are actually rectangles. In little type they all declare something like, this house is protected by so-and-so security systems. Coming from Juneau this was new for us, electronically sealed homes with silent (and not-so-silent) alarms, motion detectors, rent-a-cops scrambled by security breach messaging, and no doubt other features. One afternoon soon after moving into our new home I answered a solicitor's knock, a young woman with a broad smile and confident pitch. She was offering just to us on an un-usual basis a free electronic home security system if only we would display her company's sign on our front lawn. The advertising for her company instead of competitors would pay for the system. If neighbors asked us how much we paid, we were to say (in a conspiratorial tone), "We get a good deal." She was genu-inely surprised when I turned her down. "But it's absolutely free!" she explained again, "Why not?" I found it hard to explain.

Before moving to our new California home, our family toured the southwest deserts, camping at the parks and visiting friends along the way. It was the first time through the deserts for my two children, raised in Alaska. For me it was a return to some familiar places twenty years later. We passed southward through the Utah canyon lands and crossed the Arizona border into the red rock coun-try near the center of the world. I passed a sign pointing to Black Mesa. We drove under a pipeline carrying coal slurry. I remembered events from a dis-tant personal past, it seemed several lifetimes ago. Our route did not pass by the place where I almost died. I did not go out of our way to see.

Nearing the rim of the Grand Canyon, we stopped at an overlook main-tained by the parks. There was an interpretive sign. The sign said something like, "Look across the canyon and notice the haze. This comes from the sulfur dioxide emissions from the Navajo generating station a hundred miles to the north. The station produces electrical power for Phoenix, Las Vegas, and other cities by burning coal from Black Mesa. The public cost for reduced visibility in the Grand Canyon has been estimated at" blah blah blah. A week or so later, passing through Southern California, I called up my old father-in-law. I said, "You told me the plants were overengineered for pollution, but the smog's so predictable the park's erected an interpretive sign!" "Goddamn it," he yelled back at me over the phone, "we did design it that way! But the owners pulled the plug to cut costs and never installed the full system!"

I felt better after that call. As he is dead now just about a year, I'm especially glad I made it. I feel bad about the haze. But I see confirmed something impor-tant about massive, chaotic, unpredictable systems. Something I have come to learn in Alaska since I was that long-haired California punk who saw specks in-stead of workers. Individuals matter. Whether we live in a natural world under the thumb of chaos or beneath the eye of some unfathomable plan, it's all the same. We live under grace, unearned chances sometimes given to the living for unknown reasons. I'm a living example. And the smallest events—from butter-fly wings to locked entryways—can create large, unbelievable effects. Believing this makes all the difference.

5

Playing with Fish

Tradition and Conflict in Southwest Alaska

There's a saying, "The fish are not to be played with." This was explained to me by a Yup'ik elder in Togiak, a small community with about 840 people on the Bering Sea. It's one of many basic instructions taught to village children here and throughout southwest Alaska, a region where villages rely upon fishing and hunting. I've come to understand that the lesson is similar to instructions received by children elsewhere, such as look both ways before crossing a street, take medicine with adult supervision, and wear a bike helmet. They are commonsense lessons in survival taught to protect loved ones. And in the case of playing with fish, the saying is taught to protect nature.

The lesson about playing with fish nests within the cultural traditions of the Yup'ik Eskimo of the Bering Sea. The teaching touches on correct ways of perceiving nature. It describes how humans may find rightful places within it. Yup'ik traditions have been taught from parent to child around the Bering Sea for thousands of years. They are tested each generation within a world seasonally abundant and unforgivingly harsh. Their truth and utility are revealed by the continued survival of people in these Far Northern places.

More recently, Yup'ik traditions have received further tests and challenges from other traditions arriving to the Bering Sea region from the south. One new arrival is sport angling. By comparison with Yup'ik traditions, sport fishing is a much younger system of knowledge and practice, part of cultural traditions from Europe. Relatively new, vibrant, and expansive, sport fishing traditions also offer lessons about nature and the rightful place of humans. They are lessons of a different sort. By the design of none, these two great cultural traditions have collided in southwest Alaska. At the turn of this century, the collision was severely testing the survival of the traditional world of the Yup'ik people.

Some sport fishers detest this chapter. For this I'm sorry. I first presented these materials at a fisheries management meeting in Anchorage in 1987. The swift emotional reaction stunned me. Several infuriated sport fisheries biologists yanked me aside. I had personally insulted them, they angrily charged. My report was an unwarranted attack. Further, they accused, the report was a thinly disguised politically motivated assault on sport fishing designed to unfairly cut off anglers from public fishing waters in southwest Alaska. The rebuke left me reeling. And entirely baffled. Where did *this* come from, this emotional explosion touched off by a scientific report? It seemed to come from nowhere I had ever been.

With more experience I've come to understand that emotional outbursts in scientific meetings simply confirm that we scientists are only human too, subject to the inner impulses that drive humans everywhere. To comprehend the source of emotional, nonobjective reactions, look to the roots of personal conviction, to core values, to the areas of pure faith for the aggrieved. In this case, delve to the very roots of sport fishing traditions. There, at the core of the sport, is a high idealism. This may be the source. Many sport fishing professionals believe their sport to be unmatched. For them, the sport in its purest form is unquestionably beneficial, both to people and to fish. This is a basic tenet of faith. For true believers, a reasoned, challenging viewpoint, such as that of a Yup'ik elder, undermines the foundations of faith. As such, the challenge is disorienting, gut-wrenching, and psychologically threatening. There's an initial rush to righteous anger. Then the challenge is dismissed as self-serving politics or simple ignorance. For the faithful, it's heresy to consider it an authentic possibility.

The idealistic roots of sport fishing appear to have been planted as early as the fifteenth century. Some ascribe the origins of sport fishing to the *Treatise of Fishing with an Angle*, a short treatise written in the early 1400s by an unknown author and published in 1496 in the second *Book of St. Albans*. Oral tradition attributes the tract to Juliana Berners, by legend a sportswoman and nun at Sopwell, near the Abbey of St. Albans, twenty miles northwest of London. The treatise sets out the rules of the sport, that is, rod, line, and hook (and not nets, weirs, or traps). Sport angling is outwitting fish. The tract provides a detailed list of artificial lures, baits, and techniques specific to each variety.

But according to the treatise, angling is more than simply success in catching fish to eat. It's a sport conducted for the refinement of the participant, engendering long life, joy in the presence of nature, and other benefits to the body and soul. The sport is for the "virtuous, gentle, and freeborn," that is, for gentlemen and gentlewomen. The solitary, reflective angler, by following the rules of the game, exercises the highest virtues, including faith, hope, love, patience, humility, fortitude, knowledge, liberality, and a contented mind. Because of this, according to the treatise, sport fishing is the best and preferred among the three other noble sports—hunting, hawking, and fowling. Gentle fishers were instructed by the constitutive treatise to be well mannered and considerate of neighbors—"Break no man's hedges, nor open any man's gates without shutting them," "Do not fish in any poor man's private water without his permission and good will," and "Be not in the habit of breaking any men's fish traps lying in their weirs." But while respecting others, the treatise also encouraged self-promotion of the sport—"You should busy yourself to nourish the game in everything that you can, and to destroy all such things as are devourers of it, and all those that do according to this rule will have the blessing of God and St. Peter."

Such high idealism continues today. From such humble beginnings, sport angling has triumphed, far overshadowing hunting, hawking, and fowling in popularity. It has expanded to include group pursuits organized by big business, not just the solitary excursions of the gentle. In Alaska, the sport fishing industry supports fishing charters, fishing guides, wilderness lodges, outfitted float trips, and retail merchants of specialized fishing gear, boats, and information. Tens of thousands of visitors come to Alaska to sport fish annually, singly or as parts of charter and guided packages. There are large supporting institutions in law, biological management, and public parklands.

In Alaska, sport fishing is promoted by professionals who are at times driven by a missionary zeal. In the Alaska Department of Fish and Game, my employer for twenty-odd years, sport fish managers were taught that their legal mandate was to open up more areas to sport fishing. Funds from federal sales taxes on sport equipment were ploughed into an array of efforts. Pristine wilderness rivers were publicized. Boat ramps for public access were constructed. Rivers and lakes were stocked with game fish. Public rights to waters were fought for in court. Allocations of fish to sport anglers were tenaciously defended in fisheries management meetings. Sport fish biologists commonly followed the original precepts to a tee: to "busy yourself to nourish the game in everything that you can, and to destroy all such things as are devourers of it." Some department biologists extended this beyond natural predators to include other perceived competitors, such as commercial fishers. At times, it extended to subsistence fishers in Alaska Native villages.

Because of emerging conflicts, several subsistence researchers, including me, traveled to southwest Alaska in the mid-1980s. Subsistence fisheries and hunts were under pressure from growing commercial and sport interests. We visited Togiak, Quinhagak, and Goodnews Bay to collect information. Each village sits near the Bering Sea by the mouth of a major river. From Yup'ik experts we learned that the river drainages supported the villages. Seasonally, villagers traveled upriver to fish, hunt, and trap. Family fish camps at traditional sites stretched from the coast to the headwater lakes. The Kanektok and Arolik rivers supported Quinhagak. Togiak River supported Togiak village. The Goodnews River supported Goodnews Bay village.

We were told of growing problems with non-Native sport fishers flown in by lodges and outfitters in increasing numbers, almost all from outside Alaska. Sport fishers were encroaching on traditional net sites, displacing Yup'ik fishers. River water used for drinking in the villages was showing higher bacteria counts from upstream effluent. Vandalism was on the rise at family fish camps. Fishing regulations seemed to favor sport fishing—it remained open when subsistence and commercial fishing were closed. We documented the reported problems for presentation to government boards charged with addressing such issues. It was at this time I learned of the customary rule about playing with fish.

During the summer of 1987, problems reached a flash point when state regulators closed commercial and subsistence salmon fishing, but not sport fishing, on the lower Kanektok River during a low point in the runs. A flotilla of small riverboats from the village of Quinhagak traveled up the Kanektok River to visit sport fishing camps. The Yup'iks asked the sport fishers to stop fishing too. By and large, the sport fishers refused. Someone called in the Alaska state troopers. The confrontations made the front pages of the *Anchorage Daily News*. Heated debates filled local village council offices. In August, the Qanirtuuq tribal government at Quinhagak closed Native corporation lands along the lower Kanektok River to sport anglers. This had little effect. Anglers fished from boats and gravel bars beneath the high-water mark, areas that were considered public waters and land under state and federal laws.

In December, village residents of Quinhagak, Goodnews Bay, and Togiak sought relief from the state of Alaska. Petitions were submitted to the Alaska Board of Fisheries, a citizen board appointed by the governor to regulate Alaska's fisheries. One set of petitions proposed that the lower portions of the rivers, the areas most used by subsistence fishers, be closed to sport fishing to deal with displacement problems, but to leave the upriver areas open to sport fishing. The other petitions to the board asked for something novel—a ban on the practice of catch-and-release fishing along local rivers. It was this second request and its rationale that bedeviled the fisheries board and most infuriated highminded sport fishers.

From the view of most sport fishing guides I spoke with during my research, there were no justifiable problems between subsistence and sport fishers along the Togiak, Kanektok, and Goodnews Rivers. In their assessment, competition for resources seemed hardly an issue because the guides practiced a catch-and-release policy. Most fish were returned to the water after being caught by clients. The total number of fish actually kept in the sport fisheries was relatively small in comparison with the local subsistence and commercial fisheries.

According to the sport industry, catch-and-release was good fishery management. It was being encouraged more and more by state sport fish biologists as a way to conserve fish stocks. A representative of an Anchorage sport fishing association explained their position before the Alaska Board of Fisheries at the December meeting: "Our club is a fly-fishing club. Most members are strong in support of catch-and-release for native and transient stocks. It's against good management to require fishermen to kill a fish when they can put it back for someone else to catch. The sportsmen are not competing with subsistence. They are releasing the catch." A sport fishing lodge operator in southwest Alaska echoed this view: "We are conservative with the resource. We fish small tributaries, and we regulate the pressure in these streams. It would be difficult to fish them without wiping out the fish stock except for catch-and-release practices. About seventy-five percent of my clients want to take home salmon, species preferences depending upon the run, but all species. Of resident stocks, we keep two or less per week per client, and we return all rainbows. Each client releases an average of fifteen to thirty fish per day."

In addition to conservation, catch-and-release was a good business practice. Because of high catch rates, sport fishers would stop fishing in short order if required to keep the catch. Individual bag limits would be quickly reached. Lodges and guides would have more difficulty marketing fishing trips of shorter duration. Clientele were paying for the experience of fishing in pristine waters, not just successful fishing. Catch-and-release allowed that. It extended fishing time and recreational use days along the rivers, increasing business earnings calculated by the user day.

The sport users testifying at the fisheries board suggested that perhaps the problems with subsistence fishers stemmed from jealousy about guides making money. If so, they suggested the villages should get into the business. Or perhaps the problems were territorial, based on a mistaken notion that the local rivers belonged to them and should be closed to strangers. Perhaps it stemmed in part from prejudice against non-Natives. Or perhaps the problem was worry by local commercial fishers about competition from the growing sport industry. However, this was no real issue because of catch-and-release practices, in their assessment. The sport fishers recommended that the fisheries board take no action on the catch-and-release petitions.

From a traditional Yup'ik worldview, the fishing by strangers along local rivers appeared quite different. In the minds of many Yup'iks, the activities of sport fishers posed serious threats to the future food supply. And they created immediate conflicts with subsistence fishers, especially elders, who out of courtesy were displaced from traditional fishing sites. An elder from Goodnews Bay identified the major problems, beginning his testimony to the fisheries board in traditional fashion, by dating his first consciousness as a human being.

I first became aware of my senses in 1924 when I was three years old. At the beginning [as a youth] there was only white trading [no sport fishing]. All activity was for subsistence needs. We always brought back the subsistence catch. We never wasted anything. We stored it. We shared it with the elders and others.

The number one rule in the Yup'ik way of life is, we don't waste subsistence food, subsistence animals. You bring back whatever you catch. When this rule is broken, usually something drastic happens. Usually the one who breaks it suffers the consequences.

The subsistence catch is shared when it is put up. It is shared with the elderly and the needy.

There's been some changes since the sport fisheries came. You've heard of the saying, "You catch a fish and let it go, save it for next year." We are taught in the Yup'ik way of life, once you handle that fish, it dies once it leaves you, dies where people can't see it.

Also, the people can no longer use their traditional fish camps anymore because of the sport fishing activity along the river. They have been taken over by the sport fishermen, the good fishing spots where they catch subsistence foods. The people don't go there anymore, because they respect the [sport] people there. You don't go there. You feel obligated not to go there. These are traditional spots. They can't go back to those places.

During our research, I conducted interviews about sport fishing at Togiak, formally interviewing fifty-three people in forty-eight households about the general topic, and informally speaking with many others. We traveled up the river to observe subsistence and sport practices. We mapped fishing sites of potential conflict. From these pursuits, it became clear to me that villagers were well aware of fishing practices upriver. The activities of sport anglers in the traditional areas of the village could not help but be under scrutiny. What the villagers observed were not good conservation practices. They saw a bizarre, disturbing manner of treating fish. Anglers were catching fish and throwing them away, back into the water. This was wrong, according to one elderly woman I interviewed:

I wondered what those people were getting up the river? When my family took me upriver, I saw them up there. At this time I saw them catch fish and let it go. I wondered, are they playing around with fish? Playing around with fish is not nice because they are not meant to be played around with. Fish aren't supposed to be played with.

A middle-aged man observed the same:

When we went out for netting, we saw a couple of people catch fish and let them go and saw them keep a few for themselves. Going down from my net site, I saw a floating fish. Only half of the flesh was taken. The other half [the filleted carcass] was not. As Natives, we don't take fish and throw it away in this manner. We take it home and prepare it [the carcass] for our dogs. We don't scatter food around, because it is our food.

His wife continued,

> Those people play with the fish, and the fish will decrease. Playing with all foods
> tends to decrease them. My father used to tell us that all things of the sea and the
> land belong to God and it isn't meant to be played with. If they scatter the bones,
> they will lack food in the winter. In the wilderness, the bones not eaten by dogs are
> dug [by Yup'iks] under the ground and covered. And some bones with fish meat
> are given to the dogs.

An elderly woman confirmed this concern:

> Bones are supposed to be buried because there is a saying that fish bones aren't
> supposed to be scattered around. Probably those people do not conserve them.
> They waste them. As Yup'iks, we don't release the fish we catch.

In Togiak, many of the interviews were conducted in Yup'ik. The Yup'ik
word used for the upriver fishers was *iqsagcet*, referring to those who fish with
hook and line, those who jig for fish. The word may be translated as "anglers,"
identifying the people with a fishing technique. For Yup'iks, angling was a traditional method for capturing food to bring home and to share with family and
the elderly. Fish was a staple food, so much so that the word for "food" (*neqa*) is
the same word as for "fish." The actions of the strange anglers were considered
bizarre because food was being caught and then immediately thrown away, that
is, returned to the water. The "number one rule"—bring home the food you
catch—was being broken.

Why would someone do this? The Yup'ik of southwest Alaska were familiar enough with the Euro-American sport fishing ethic to understand that this
activity was a form of recreation for non-Native visitors. The phrase offered by
villagers, "playing around with fish," expressed that understanding in part. The
Yup'ik verb used to describe the activities of non-Native anglers was *naanguar*,
which refers to playing with toys or playing with objects as if toys, like a child
plays with a flashlight on a rainy day. The verb expresses the imputed motiva-
tion for catching and throwing away food: the anglers play with fish as if they
were toys, for the fun of it.

This understanding evoked a strong social and moral condemnation from
villagers. It was an improper way to treat fish and food. This was a basic rule

learned by children at an early age. Many expressed it, illustrated by these four persons.

> Food is not meant to be played with. What they catch, they should bring back to those who can't get fish themselves.

> They should split and hang them for food in the winter, not make fun, not playing around with them. When I take kids upriver, I tell them not to play with the fish.

> As Yup'iks, we don't play around with fish. What we catch we hang under the caches to dry or store.

> Do not waste fish. When caught, take care of the food in the way it's meant to be taken care of. Either dry it up or freeze it if freezers are available. Or split the fish and dry it in the Yup'ik way of drying. Or if not, give the caught fish to a Yup'ik person who can split the fish and dry the fish.

These statements about the proper treatment of food were emphatic and emotional. Potential social and health consequences for violating these proscriptions were of great concern, due to an underlying view of nature.

For the Yup'iks of southwest Alaska, the natural world of animals and plants is filled with a conscious awareness of how humans treat them. Animals are not just like persons; they are persons in their own right. Beneath the physical form of coho, sockeye, or char are living beings capable of keen perception, thought, emotion, and powerful action. The salmon that return to be fished and used by people do so under a conscious will. The natural world is layered, with subtleties, complexities, and mysteries. As I understand things, each individual fish may have a will and consciousness. And for each fish stock or type there may be a consciousness, like that of a master or keeper. And all fish, like all living things, fall beneath the ultimate conscious sway of *Ellam Yua*, the one Great Person of the Universe, the Yup'ik word for God. The natural world is filled with beings in human and animal forms. Humans are careful how to use sockeye or coho or char so the living beings who control the fish will let them return to be used in the future.

Playing with a particular fish was considered "abuse" by those I interviewed. It was a serious disrespect to the living beings of the fish. Playing with fish was viewed as inflicting unwarranted pain and distress with which humans should empathize.

It is not us they [sport fishers] are abusing, it is the fish they are abusing. After they damage the mouths, they let them go. It is like us: when the fish are hurt, they can't eat.

As Yup'iks, we don't like to see fish hurt. Probably the hurt fish gets bad. When *we* are hurting, it's not good. Probably it's not good for the fish either. As human beings, *we* hurt, and when the fish are hurt, it may sting. Fish hurt like that.

A fish getting cut is the same as with a person. Cuts get infected, just like when you get cut with a knife. It's the same as with fish.

Within this set of beliefs, Yup'iks understand fish to be sentient, feeling beings like humans, who respond to injury and pain like humans. This is clearly at odds with the understanding of fish underlying catch-and-release practices, where there is concern for the life of the fish but no substantial empathy or concern for the feelings of the fish or for the pain inflicted by being hooked multiple times.

According to Yup'iks, such abuse perverts the natural order. In a healthy, natural world, the fish are plentiful, whole, and fat for drying, smoking, and eating. Abuse of fish by humans distorts the manifest world, creating observable abnormalities. Fish become sickly, skinny, and ugly. Many I spoke with observed that this was beginning to happen to fish in the Togiak River.

Ever since there have been sport fishermen, the people have caught skinny fish. The flesh is not well built, except the head. The trouts [char] especially. Some of the reds, chums, and kings as well. Ever since, that's what they [villagers] have been catching. I believe the playing with fish may be the cause of the fish that are getting skinny. Their mouths are torn. The people do not like to handle the ones that are skinny. The fish don't look appetizing. They go to their dogs, not into their caches or refrigerators.

When elders or we fishermen ourselves are out fishing at the bay, we don't like to catch a fish damaged or abused. Sometimes no eyes, or one eye on the fish, or scratched up. We don't like to see or catch fish that are abused in the body when fishing for food.

We know about letting fish go [after being hooked]. Some fish go swimming with one eye. And we see fresh fish dead on the bottom of rivers. I had a net on the beach. There was a fresh trout in the net. Its eye was gone. So I brought it to the house. It was suffering. That is why the fish are decreasing.

We don't like the fisherman upriver because they abuse fish. They catch it, tear the mouths, and some die. As elders, we don't like them to do this. Fish die off if played with.

At a town meeting in Quinhagak, one elder instructed people to inspect fish for torn mouths and not to eat them. Those fish would be sick. Eating them might spread sickness to the people.

Abusing living beings ultimately leads to their decrease. This is a natural effect known and stated by many. Animals get sick, waste away, and die off. The waste of food by humans inevitably leads to such decreases.

Living beings become aware of waste in subtle ways, especially through their unused carcasses and bones touched by humans. One elder explained that it's like touching the lens of eyeglasses: fingerprints are left that can be seen when the glass is held to the light. When fish and bones are touched, it's like that. Fish will not swim past the bones or carcasses of fish that have been touched and discarded by people. Because of this, special care is necessary in disposing of the bones of fish or fish carcasses.

I've heard, as Yup'iks, we are not supposed to scatter bones or fish.

My mother told me not to play with fish or scatter fish around.

The word used here was *eskavte*, meaning "to scatter about in disarray." Bones and carcasses touched by people must be dried, eaten, or fed to dogs. If not used this way, they should be buried in the ground or otherwise properly disposed. If touched carcasses and bones are scattered about, thrown in the water so they are seen lying around, then the fish will not return.

My father used to say, when there is a stinky fish in the water, the fish don't swim around that area. But that's only when human beings cause them to be lying around. It's all right after they lay their eggs because birds feed on them.

When you clean fish, you don't throw the bones in the main river. You bury them in the ground or feed them to the dogs, because the fish go by them. Do not burn them either. However, you can put them in the lake [Togiak Lake]. The old [spawned out] fish themselves are up there after the spawning runs.

We don't like bones caught in the nets. We put the bones under the ground. This is because the bones keep the fish away if put in the river. When I go upriver, I don't like to see bones and rotting fish. We take a shovel upriver with us to put bones under the ground.

Assessed by these principles, the catch-and-release practice becomes a particularly blatant and dangerous form of waste, for the unused fish are put back into the water, some to become sick and distorted, others sinking to the bottom in death, the bones exuding the telltale essence of human misconduct for all fish beings to see. Some villagers sought ways to mitigate the severity of the practice. One suggested to me that instead of wasting fish, the sport anglers should leave the fish on the sand bars for the wild animals or birds to feed on. At least then some use would be achieved and the fish bones kept from the water. Two women I spoke with felt compelled to clean up after the sport fishers.

When we saw the dead fish, we picked them up and dried them out.

I have seen lots of dead fish along the banks and in the clear water downriver from the sport camp. I went up last year in July and saw these. It upset me. I picked some of them and cut their heads and used them so they wouldn't waste. But there were lots more I couldn't use.

Clearly, there is an essential, irreconcilable contradiction between the worldviews of catch-and-release sport anglers and of traditional Yup'iks. What is understood to be good resource management and business practices in the one tradition is understood as dangerous abuse of the natural world in the other, leading to the destruction of life in the river. The traditional Yup'ik view can be summed up by the statement of one elder.

Long time ago there is a saying: If you play with the fish, this decreases them. The fish will decrease where there are no more.

It's good to believe that mutual understanding helps lead to mutual accommodations among human groups. I believe this. I try to practice this. But many of my good friends say I'm naive.

It's of interest to me that the petitions to the fisheries board from the Yup'iks offered accommodations for non-Native anglers. Despite the extensive problems faced by local fishers, the grassroots petitions carved out places for the newcomers along the rivers. The proposals to close the lower rivers to sport fishing were designed to help the Yup'ik elders who made day trips to net sites.

But they also provided places for sport anglers to fish. Under this plan, the upper river would have been open to the sport and subsistence fishers alike. The Alaska Board of Fisheries rejected these proposals. However, in response, the state board passed an alternative regulation. The board prohibited sport fishing within three hundred feet of a subsistence net. If a net was encountered, sport anglers must defer to the net. As I write, this regulation is still in effect.

The other Yup'ik petitions to prohibit the practice of catch-and-release fishing also included accommodations for visiting sport anglers. Under the proposal, sport angling was still allowed. However, a specific variant of sport fishing was to be disallowed, the catching and releasing of fish. All people were to be treated equally in this matter. Every fisher would be required to keep the fish caught, whether subsistence or sport fishing.

You may correctly guess that the catch-and-release proposal was strenuously opposed by sport fishing professionals. It also was strenuously opposed by the sport fish biologists of my department. You can imagine the arguments against this regulatory change. The sport fish biologists said scientific data existed on catch-and-release mortalities, and they were acceptable (at least to sport fish biologists). Further, wilderness lodges and sport guides would be put out of business. Future opportunities for sport guiding businesses by the Yup'iks would be foreclosed. Prohibiting catch-and-release had never been done before. It would set a bad precedent. Further, catch-and-release was good conservation. "And by the way," it was whispered to me, "fish don't feel much pain. Nor do they have spirits." "And," it was not whispered to me, "you've personally attacked us with your biased report."

You may also correctly guess that the fisheries board did not prohibit catch-and-release on the three rivers in southwest Alaska. In fact, since the proposals, over the last decade or so, the state board has been expanding catch-and-release requirements to more and more stocks and rivers. The conversion of the sport of angling, from catching an outwitted fish to eat, to catching fish purely for fun and profit, is well underway in Alaska. When I left the Fish and Game Department, sport fish managers were still toying with the idea of public education in rural areas to explain the virtues of catch-and-release fishing. Under this plan, in true missionary zeal, the public educators wait out the traditional elders (who eventually must die) and convert the children. Cooption has been another trend. Native villages in western Alaska have been poor and cash strapped. Commercial fishing has been on a downturn. Enticement of village corporations into the business of guided sport fishing established new bulwarks protecting catch-and-release practices.

I would like to believe that the troubles of Yup'ik villagers in southwest Alaska have lessened since these conflicts were first debated before the state fisheries board. Perhaps displacement of elders has actually lessened. However, given other trends, I expect the catch-and-release problem has become increasingly convoluted and intractable. In the villages, the Yup'iks still teach their children. In the cities, sport professionals teach theirs. It's an uneasy multiculturalism where contradictory practices are put together, as on the pristine waters in Yup'ik homelands.

Still, I wonder yet about the legend of Juliana Berners and the medieval treatise on sport fishing framing the early idealism at the beginnings of the sport. I wonder about the parts concerning gentle persons and courtesy toward neighbors where you fish. About closing gates. And nonencroachment. And the high virtues exercised by angling—love, humility, liberality, among others. I wonder, when were these lost to sport fishing? Or, if the highest ideals of the sport are still alive, then I wonder, how might they be practiced? Especially, how might they be practiced in southwest Alaska? For here they are basic matters of survival for humans and for nature. Whether or not you believe in spirits.

6

Perfect Symphony

Classical Music in Unexpected Places

The Juneau Symphony Orchestra, established in 1962. We chuckle a little. In Juneau, Alaska, a small town with about thirty thousand people hugging the North Pacific coast, framed by ice fields, drenched by constant rain, approachable only by boat or plane, there's a symphony orchestra. It's hard being too pretentious in Alaska. Alaskans know what they have and know what they don't. And they don't have Paganini. The recruitment standards of the Juneau Symphony Orchestra were reasonable, considering. "How to Become a Player" is posted on their website. It simply says, "Musicians are welcome to come to rehearsals on Tuesdays (locations TBA) at 7 P.M. to begin playing with the orchestra." Just like that. When we attend the Juneau Symphony, we come out to hear our neighbors play—a nurse practitioner on cello, an office worker on flute, a wilderness guide on violin, a woodworker on double bass. They are simple volunteers filling symphonic positions, doggedly giving their all. They play for those who can hear the strains of something true. And we all turn out to hear at the high school auditorium.

Last week, we were pulling into the California Center for the Performing Arts in Escondido, north of San Diego. We were arriving to hear the San Diego Symphony Orchestra, a somewhat different organization. Finding a parking place among the rows of polished cars, I remembered how we arrived at Juneau Symphony performances, by sliding downhill. The high school sat on the corner a block from home. We'd walk in blowing rain, in boot-deep slush, sliding over slick ice, minutes away from front-center seats. Our neighbors came much

the same way, bundled in foul-weather gear. We attended, Sylvia and I, without our two children. They're such complainers. They throw hissy fits about
the symphony, for them a pure torture. In genuine sympathy they mourned the
fates of their neighbors, the poor DeCherney kids, who *always* had to go. So,
accordingly, we coerce ours to concerts just occasionally, to prime, rather than
irreparably crush, their delicate sensitivities.

You must understand that Sylvia is a patron of the arts. She needs classical
music like plants need light. She must listen to it regularly, without fail, during each week, or she fades. She cross-stitches on the couch while the music
plays. She has been expanding her record collection, benefiting from the pell-
mell rush to CDs. She hears classical, romantic, and baroque, some modern,
a little Renaissance, especially ballets, symphonies, and piano concertos; old
compositions given life through two speakers across the living room, giving life
to Sylvia.

She must hear live concerts too. In Juneau, the classical season plays in the
dark of the northern winter when life's ebb is lowest. Downhill we'd slip and
slide to the school auditorium, a murky glow in the rainy dark. Sometimes the
school gets double booked with a classical concert and basketball game on the
same night. Then the indoor commons is bustling with concertgoers peeling
left to the auditorium and sport fans in baseball caps and jerseys peeling right
to the gym. With both doors ajar, you can stand in the commons sipping Coke
and listen to a fast-break layup blend with Debussy. Why not?

The classics evoke high aspirations. In music, it's a search for perfect symphony, that special place, that occasional moment when it's almost possible
to hear a celestial chord, the music of the spheres. The classics also evoke a
type of sophistication, some may say pretension, for the erudite and exclusive.
True ballet, it may be said, is experienced only in Europe, real Tchaikovsky
only in Russia. Reproductions abound but the authentic classics, they say, the
Great Performances, are found in particular places and at special times. At the
other extreme, the classics invite aspirations (or pretensions) of another sort,
an enthusiasm for cultivating class in the least expected places, such as on the
Alaskan frontier. It's the *can do* enthusiasm of the Far North. Yes, a symphony
orchestra in Juneau! The high sophisticates just cluck their tongues and smile.

It's hard to deny there sometimes were white-knucklers when something was
not quite right with the Juneau Symphony, where tightly gripping the bottom
of the seat helped ease you through a passage. The clarinets, usually. But in
my truthful assessment, the discomforting moments were diminishing. And the

crowds grew larger each season. What was happening to us? Was the symphony maturing? Kyle Wiley Pickett, the latest conductor, promoted the symphony around town with full-sized, stand-up, foam-core cutouts of himself, grinning and conducting in rain gear. He explained it to me over dinner. Enticing someone to that first performance was the challenge. Americans don't normally think of classical music because they don't know it. But if you can get them through the door, they come back. They like what they hear. Perhaps. Whatever it was, Juneau was turning out. We came to hear Dvořák, Respighi, Vivaldi, and Tchaikovsky reproduced by neighbors in the midwinter dark of the Far North, to cheer this rustic symphony with standing ovations, even the young moms with fussy babies in the rear cry room.

We observe a somewhat different decorum at the California Center for the Performing Arts in Escondido. We quietly move among a different crowd, gathering to hear the San Diego Symphony. From the parking lot there is muted, indirect lighting. A warm night wind wafts from the California desert with hints of coastal sage and orange. Long dresses and black coats whisk across the polished paving stones. Limousines drop off patrons with flashes of chrome.

As we move toward the door, Sylvia is shielding her eyes.

"What's wrong?"

"Migraine," she whimpers softly.

"Oh, no, when?"

"On the freeway."

"Should we go?"

"No, I want to hear the Mussorgsky."

"With a headache?"

"There's no pain. It's just . . . weird. Maybe they'll play it first and we can leave."

The arts center towers above us, broad windows with chandeliers casting gold on the stairways. We enter with the flow along polished flagstone hallways, accepting programs from the door keeps. Unfortunately, the program says Mussorgsky is last. With a tip to an obliging bar master we preorder espresso and tea for the intermission in case we make it that far.

"How're you doing?" I ask as we stroll toward the hall.

"OK."

"Any pain?"

"No. Just weirdness."

The ushers point us to an aisle on the concert hall floor toward the front.

Ranks of seats rise steeply about us, curtained private boxes over the stage, brass-banistered sections hanging above us in the upper airs, filling with patrons. The night's formal attire features blacks and dark browns, heavy coats, large jewelry, and silver hair. There's coughing, some winter malady afflicting the elderly. The program offers free cough drops. We settle into our seats.

"Pretty close," I say, glancing at Sylvia.

She seems to be ducking beneath her left arm.

"What's wrong?"

"Mothballs," she mumbles through her sleeve.

"What?"

"Mothballs."

She nods at a silver-haired matron standing at the seat directly in front of us, wrapped in a fur-lined coat.

"She's had it in mothballs. Can't you smell it?"

"Barely. It's your migraine. You're hypersensitive. I think it's perfume."

"Augh! We can't sit here."

"Just breathe through your hand."

"I can't sit through the concert breathing through my hand! She's drenched in it, whatever it is! This *will* give me a headache."

Working our way back across the seats of well-dressed patrons, we approach our usher. We must find the head usher to change seats, she explains. As musicians warm up onstage we find the busy head usher, who, without missing a step, leads us to new seats buffered by empties beneath gently vented crosscurrents.

"He didn't blink an eye," I remark.

"This is good," says Sylvia, looking to her left, "we're close to a door."

We begin with *Sensemaya*, by Silvestre Revueltas, an Afro-Cuban chant to kill a snake. The program bills it as an orgiastic seven-minute tone poem of asymmetric jungle rhythms with explosions of brass and strings. *Tap TAP tap tap*—the percussion lightly begins, slowly building with a contrapuntal pulse. I look over at Sylvia. Her head is tilting away from the front. Her wrist is draped across the facing ear. Her eyes shut tight.

"How's it going?"

"OK," she whimpers.

"Does it hurt?"

"No."

The uneven beat grows louder, acquiring maracas, gourds, *raspadors*, with spiky outbursts from the woodwinds. The music gathers energy to a rhythmic pounding that fills the hall, louder, louder, then, as promised, great explosions of sound from the brass and strings like blocks falling on the crowd, huge, intense detonations ending with a final blast. The theater politely applauds the slaughtered snake.

Sylvia looks dead.

"You OK?"

"Yeah," she whispers. She doesn't move for a minute.

Beethoven's Piano Concerto in C Minor follows like balm, offering long, sonorous movements and soft trilling. Sylvia drifts through it with eyes closed.

Halftime. We collect our drinks and sit in a corner away from the brighter lights and babble. At the warning flicker we file back to our seats. Oddly, other patrons surround us. Where'd they all come from? One pair has opera glasses, sweeping the stage as if searching for the enemy. A bald-headed codger in a waistcoat hops from seat to seat, peering up, muttering about drafts. A mildly perfumed couple zooms in and parks to our left beneath the eye of a frustrated usher.

The Mussorgsky begins, "Pictures at an Exhibition," Ravel's orchestration. It's one of Sylvia's favorites, ten musical portraits joined by a powerful promenade theme. The trumpet opens, then the full brass. The hall fills with sound. Sylvia hunkers down. She knows this piece. She can survive the grand opening, knowing the promise of softer variations to come. They do come, like flowing watercolors.

"HAAHOCK!"

Sylvia flinches like she's been hit. What the . . .?

"HAAHOCK!"

The sound explodes again beside her head. A looming, barrel-chested shape has materialized from nowhere right behind her. It's the cougher from hell.

"HAAHOCK!"

Every few moments the dark shape explodes by her head.

"HAAHOCK!"

Pianissimo or più sostenuto—

"HAAHOCK!"

Sylvia sprawls inert.

"HAAHOCK!"

"Sylvia?"

There's no response. The strings begin to build, chasing the lead of high flutes. A major promenade is coming. Without a sound, Sylvia gracefully arises from her seat and floats toward the exit. With a spectral quality, she disappears through the swinging doors.

"HAAHOCK!"

I'm alone. She doesn't return. A portrait ends. So, I too silently rise, unobtrusively drift toward the exit, and push through the doors.

And there's Sylvia. She's leaning against the wall, eyes closed, in that small, odd-chambered space made by the two sets of double doors, one to the concert hall and the other to the stairs. It's very dark, dimly lit by green exit lights. A muffled Mussorgsky filters through the closed doors.

"Are you OK?"

She does not move, propped against the wall. She does not open her eyes. But she is smiling.

"This is perfect," she whispers.

And she holds up a slender finger.

I wait.

The muffled music is playing.

"Shh . . ." It's barely a whisper from her. "This is the best part."

And in her face, I see it's true.

7 Profiting

How Juneau Said No to War Bucks

The news stunk. At least to me it did. News releases from the Office of the Governor flitted across my desk several times each week. Daily news logs. They kept state grunts like me abreast of the governor's policies. And this one stunk.

News Release, February 1, 1988, Juneau

COWPER PRAISES HOME-PORTING ANNOUNCEMENT

Gov. Steve Cowper welcomed today's announcement from Washington, D.C., that the U.S. Navy is considering home-porting two cruisers in Alaska in the next 18 months to two years. The Governor was notified this morning that the federal government has allocated $2.5 million to conduct an environmental impact statement regarding the basing of the two vessels in Alaska. No decision has been made about the port where the ships will be based. "This is good news for Alaska," Cowper said. "My administration is prepared to lend whatever support is necessary to prove to the Navy that Alaska is an important and suitable base for its ships. Alaska enjoys a long tradition of friendly relations with the military and I extend our good neighbor policy to these two ships." Each of the cruisers is 529 feet long, weighs 9,500 tons and is staffed by 450 sailors.

State of Alaska, Office of the Governor.

Already in Alaska's two largest urban centers, Anchorage and Fairbanks, one in ten worked for the Army or Air Force. Now it was the Navy. My family roots sink deeply into Anabaptist peace traditions. I knew my opinions lay far beyond the mainstream sentiments on this issue.

A month later, two more notices crossed my desk. The news worsened. Several phrases caught my eye: "a new era in the history of the military here," "a boost to Alaska's stumbling economy," and then an astonishing sum— "$100,000,000."

Navy Still to Decide if Alaska Fits the Bill

Within the next several weeks, planners from the Navy's Pacific Fleet will start visiting coastal cities in Alaska as part of a $2.5 million study of whether it makes military and economic sense to build a new home port here for Navy warships. It's a complicated task that will take months. The only existing naval facility in Alaska is the Naval Air Station on Adak Island in the Aleutians. Some of the cities under consideration have nothing more in place than a small boat harbor and a lone dock for visiting cruise ships. Alaska officials see the project as a boost to Alaska's stumbling economy. If Alaska helps the Navy finance a new port, it will mark a new era in the history of the military here. So far, there's been virtually no debate in Juneau on the issue. At a teleconference hearing of the House Finance Committee last Friday, Democrats and Republicans alike spoke in favor of the idea. There has been little opposition to the homeport idea in the various communities, and some local governments have gone on record in recent days supporting it.

—Article by David Hulen, *Anchorage Daily News*, March 8, 1988

Joint Resolution, March 18, 1988, Juneau

RELATING TO ESTABLISHING A UNITED STATES NAVY HOMEPORT
IN ALASKA.

Be it resolved that the Governor and the Alaska State Legislature strongly urge the United States Navy to consider establishing a homeport at one or more Alaskan communities; and be it further resolved that the State of Alaska is willing to seriously consider investment of as much as $100,000,000, through a cooperative arrangement with the United States Navy, to develop infrastructure or other capital improvements necessary for the establishment of a major, long-term Navy homeport in Alaska.

House Committee Substitute for the Committee Substitute for Senate Joint Resolution No. 55 (Rules), 15th Legislature, 2nd Session, Passed

35–1

One hundred million dollars! My legislature, Democrat and Republican alike, on record, was trying to lure the Navy into Alaska by investing up to one hundred million dollars? Surely someone misplaced a decimal point. "So far, there has been virtually no debate in Juneau on the issue," reported Dave Hulen. What's wrong with everybody?

"I hate this," I groused, flipping the newspaper to a friend at the table. It was a homeport article. Consultants predicted million-dollar payrolls if the Navy chose Juneau.

Several of us sipped coffee at the New Orpheum Theater, Juneau's tiny, dingy art theater and coffeehouse near the downtown wharf. We converged on Sunday afternoons to the Orpheum to read, as soon as the Sunday's *Anchorage Daily News* descended into town by plane and was purchased at the corner liquor store. The *Juneau Empire*, our thin local paper, had no Sunday edition. If someone was feeling flush, he unloaded the massive *New York Times* on a table. In Alaska, that's like the foreign press. We dubbed our gathering "The Reading," a weekly event of friends and nodding acquaintances, self-styled intellectuals, oddballs, frontier runabouts, mostly unmarried and unattached.

"Why?" asked the friend.

"It's just wrong."

Since spring, Juneau had caught the homeport lust. Juneau's Economic Development Council, a civic entity charged with municipal development, had earmarked and already spent thirty thousand dollars to lure the Navy into Juneau. Choose us for your homeport, they propositioned, throwing out the town's money to woo the military in the name of economic development, meaning local jobs and payrolls.

"Why is it wrong?" he asked, blandly.

"It's the military! They're trying to make money from the military!"

"What's wrong with that?"

He looked at me blankly, clueless about my sputtering anger. And I thought, "What *am* I sputtering about?" I don't even make sense to friends at the Orpheum.

I remember stomping out in frustration, wading home in a downpour of self-disgust, composing letters in my head. It was a watershed moment. I never wrote letters. But it didn't seem right. No one was objecting. No one seemed to notice any problems. And as much as anything, I felt consumed to articulate what was bugging me.

I learned that you drove letters to the *Juneau Empire*, submitting them across a reception desk. The newspaper building sits beside the fish hatchery, right on the channel, a center of empire. It's pretty smelly in August following the salmon runs. Black, stinking carcasses of pink and silver salmon rot on the flats by the thousands. Eagles, gulls, and seals congregate for feasts, looking drunk from overgorging. The receptionist smiled, verified my name and address, and took it. They published it that week, Juneau's first homeport letter.

Homeporting for Economic Opportunity a Wrong Move

To the *Juneau Empire*

August 18, 1988

Dear Editor:

"Homeporting" as an economic development opportunity is wrong for Juneau. Why? Because it is morally wrong. Homeporting as economic development creates profound ethical problems. It should not receive community support. The moral issue is this: it is wrong to want to make personal monetary profits from war or the preparation for war. It is wrong for the individual, it is wrong for the community. It is wrong to willingly choose to make money from war.

The homeport development option raises this moral issue because the reasons being given for wanting Naval ships to homeport in Juneau are economic reasons: "to make money for the community," "to bring jobs to the community," "to bol-ster the economy of the community." The reasons are not military reasons, such as strategic advantage in deployment of troops and firepower. The reasons are that Juneau can profit from a piece of the annual federal appropriation to the military. These are mercenary reasons. They display a willing eagerness to earn monetary profits from the sad reality of modern military preparedness. We as a community should resist this line of thinking, this motive, this desire. It would mean that our motivations in regard to the military would turn into economic ones. And this is a dangerously dehumanizing shift—changing our view of the military into that of a business.

If the reasons for choosing to homeport in Juneau are strategic reasons, then let's discuss these. If Juneau's location has indispensable advantages for the ap-propriate defense of the Lower 48 or Alaska, then let's discuss these. If housing tactical nuclear weapons is necessary for Juneau because of geographic or socio-political reasons, then let's discuss these. These are appropriate kinds of discus-sions in regard to homeporting. But if the motive is money, and primarily money, then this exceeds the ethical bounds of what warfare and the participation in the preparation for warfare should be about. Our community should resist this way of choosing.

The people who live in Juneau as a whole love Juneau and Southeast Alaska. They love its mix of peoples and cultures. Its high moral standards. Its productive mix of industries — fishing, state service, mining, tourism, forestry, subsistence, commerce, and others. Economic development is important for most of Juneau's residents. Choosing the best routes of economic development is an important task. In those choices, let us choose wisely, with our eyes open. And let us choose from the highest moral motives. If homeporting in Juneau is being done for monetary reasons, then it is a profound moral problem. It is ethically wrong. It is wrong for us. Sincerely,

Robert J. Wolfe

Juneau

That was that. A fringe position, I knew. But I'd gotten it off my chest. I was done with homeports.

"I saw your letter."

I heard this several times over the next few days, buttonholed on the streets of Juneau, at Foodland, in the Orpheum.

"I saw your letter."

Things rumble around places like Juneau. It's tiny. Landlocked. Overly educated. We don't have much to keep us occupied. Letters get read. You're likely to know authors. You can run into them and say what you feel.

"Thanks for writing that letter."

Things were rumbling around.

"What are we going to do next?" a middle-aged woman asked me later that week, her face pinched with worry, a woman I knew from the Methodist-Presbyterian church, never a part of the Orpheum crowd.

What did she mean, "we"? What did she mean, "do next"?

Juneau's a political town, the state's capital, in and out of the legislature session. And things had been rumbling around even before that homeport letter, maybe because of the thirty thousand dollars spent by Juneau's Economic Development Council. On schedule, the town's assembly met that week. The Navy homeport materialized on its agenda.

"Are you going to the assembly meeting?" several people asked me.

"Uh, no. I'm traveling," I said. I was off to do research in a village. I'd never even been to an assembly meeting.

"Can we read your letter?"

The Assembly of the City and Borough of Juneau has an ear for rumblings, ways of listening for slight tremors in the civic fundament, and solid, time-tested ways of responding. The assembly came prepared for its agenda. After public testimony, the assembly quickly considered and passed a resolution, dated August 22, filled with a great many *whereases* (to set the factual record straight should there be misunderstandings), and an important *therefore*:

A Resolution Calling for an Advisory Ballot Proposition

Whereas, the City and Borough of Juneau is one of eleven communities in Alaska currently being studied by the United States Navy for its potential as a site for a "homeport," and *whereas*, at this point in its decision process, the Navy has not determined the size of the proposed homeport facility or the number or types of vessels that would be assigned to the installation, and *whereas*, the best information available at this time indicates that the proposed homeport would serve two ships and that between 500 and 1,000 uniformed personnel and 100 direct civilian employees would staff the homeport and the ships, and *whereas*, as a rough comparison, the population impact of the homeport would be approximately two to four times the size of the current U.S. Coast Guard and National Guard presence in Juneau, and *whereas*, the city and borough is currently involved in the Navy homeport site evaluation process, and *whereas*, prior to the commitment and expenditure of additional municipal resources on this project, the Assembly has determined that it would be appropriate to ask the voters whether they are supportive of the city and borough continuing the site evaluation process with the Navy;

Now, therefore, be it resolved by the Assembly of the City and Borough of Juneau, Alaska: 1. Submission of Proposition to Voters. The proposition set forth in section 2 of this resolution shall be submitted to the qualified voters of the city and borough at the next regular election to be held on October 4, 1988. *2. Proposition.* The proposition to be submitted to the voters as required by section 1 shall read substantially as follows: "Advisory proposition on whether the city and borough should continue to pursue information regarding the proposed development of a Navy homeport in Juneau and continue the efforts necessary to keep Juneau in contention as a possible site.

City and Borough of Juneau, Resolution 1329

So citizens would be allowed to weigh in on the homeport issue, to advise the city on moving forward. The *Juneau Empire* covered the breaking news:

Homeport: Voters to be Asked Whether
They Favor Luring Navy

Voters will be asked in October whether they want to continue the push to lure a Navy homeport to Juneau. That decision was made Monday when the Juneau City-Borough Assembly approved a ballot question to forward to local residents in the October 4 municipal election. Juneau is one of eleven communities competing for the right to house the base, which consultants said would add hundreds of jobs and millions of dollars in payroll to the local economy.

It was clear Monday, however, that not everyone likes the idea of a homeport in Juneau. Several people objected to the wording on the ballot question, saying the language is cleverly designed to win a "yes" vote. Assembly member McKie Campbell, who helped write the ballot question, acknowledged that the language was indeed drafted to generate a positive response from the public. He noted, however, that the ballot proposition is only an advisory vote and calls for a second election when more details of the Navy plan are known. A final decision on the homeport would be up to voters at that time.

During public debate on the proposal, audience member Elaine Schroeder said the outcome of the advisory proposition could be misinterpreted. She and other audience members suggested voters should simply be asked, yes or no, if they want a homeport in Juneau. Another audience member, Rob Bosworth, read a letter to the editor published last week in the Juneau Empire. The author of the letter, Robert J. Wolfe, argued that the homeport should be rejected because it is morally wrong to pin economic development on war or the preparation for war. Mayor Ernie Polley, an ardent supporter of the homeport push, said he and other backers of the Navy base respected Wolfe's philosophical argument.

U.S. Sen. Ted Stevens, R-Alaska, at a press conference in Juneau, said he believed the Navy will announce that seven cities are still in the running, then narrow the list to three early next year. Stevens said he believed Juneau and Ketchikan would both make the list of seven cities.

— Article by Bruce Scandling, *Juneau Empire*, August 23, 1988

The managing editor of the *Juneau Empire* weighed in the following day. That ear was also to the ground, listening. The paper had the first say on the referendum:

Public to Have a Say on Homeport

Monday night, Juneau City-Borough Assembly member Rosalee Walker described a proposed ballot question on the Navy homeport as a "pig in a poke." That's exactly what it is. No one knows enough about the effects of basing a Navy ship here to make a definitive judgment on it. We do, however, know one thing: If a ship were based here, upwards of 500 Navy personnel and their families would move into our community, making dramatic changes. Beyond that, the rest is conjecture.

With $30,000 in public money already invested in the homeport project, it's time taxpayers were asked what they thought. If the vast majority of local voters do not want a Navy ship based here under any circumstances, then the community would be best off dropping the matter now. If, on the other hand, voters support the effort for basing a ship here, then the October balloting will serve as an endorsement, demonstrating to the Navy that it would be welcome in the Capital City.

We respectfully disagree with those who want to wait for more information, or who believe the community should not be stirred up until more information is available. It is better to get the community stirred up now and let the chips fall where they may than to wait to find out if Juneau is chosen to debate the issue. Those who support a homeport in Juneau, including this newspaper, have made no secret of it. Thousands of others, however, have not had an opportunity to speak. This ballot issue will afford them that opportunity. It would not be wise to delay a referendum, because sooner or later the homeport issue will be debated in public. The sooner that happens, the better.

> Managing editor of the *Juneau Empire*, editorial, *Juneau Empire*,
> August 24, 1988

So the *Empire* launched the public debate, almost with a chortle. "Get the community stirred up!" "Let the chips fall where they may!" And the managing editor announced the paper's position: the *Empire* supported the Navy homeport. It was good economics for the community. And, I expect, good print. Papers would sell well.

The next few Readings at the Orpheum were like none before. By word of mouth they grew in size, energy, and volume. Boisterous newcomers sat or stood, crunched among the usual readers around benches in the dingy coffeehouse, hovering over tables piled with Sunday newspapers. Some I knew, others I didn't. The Reading began attracting hoary politicos, still waging old personal battles, and a number of wide-eyed, eager young activists. No one pretended to read. The Old Left railed against government, America, capitalism, and history, buoyant on this new platform. Greenies thumped passionately about wilderness protection and secret submarine tests in the fjords. Slow-growth advocates worried over losing Juneau's charm and small-town values. The ideological mash mixed, heated, distilled, while the Orpheum sold vats of coffee. It all tasted a bit strange to me. These were not exactly Anabaptist peacemakers. Not a one. But, they were neighbors. And really, not a bad bunch.

I think some thought something was being organized, a movement, a political action group, a party. But it seemed rather free-form to me. No clear leaders as yet. People coming and going. If there was a "plan," it was only this: Write letters to the *Juneau Empire*. Keep 'em simple. Focus on concerns. Concerns differed—that was OK. Just voice them. Keep it in the news. And above all, say nothing, absolutely nothing, disparaging about servicemen. That was a suicide pill.

Some itched for more action. Writing letters seemed, well, prosaic. A small group coalesced in a corner and announced it would collect signatures for a political ad saying, "We don't want a homeport." They would place it the *Juneau Empire* just before the vote, paid by donations. They also pledged to testify at public meetings on the homeport issue, if any were scheduled. That was it. The Grand Strategy. Grassroots. Cheap. And fundamentally naïve. At the time, none had researched Navy homeports or their track records. We were unburdened by the historic fact that no city had ever turned one down.

Troubling Questions About Homeporting

To the *Juneau Empire*
September 15, 1988
Dear Editor:

Among the many problems I have with the idea of a Navy base in Juneau (increased loads on the city's social services, the possibility of nuclear weapons in my front yard, the elimination of many nearby outdoor recreational opportunities, etc.), one stands out: the possibility that political decisions with profound effects on this community will be made in Washington, D.C., and/or by people with little or no long-term commitment to the quality of life here. Members of the city-borough assembly and the Juneau Economic Development Council who are subtly force-feeding "homeporting" (what a cozy word!) to us should be asked why they are so eager to sell Juneau's soul for a few bucks. I won't begin to believe they're even slightly motivated by true patriotism until they know—and can explain to the rest of us—why a Navy base in Juneau would be strategically important to the nation's defense.

Sincerely,

John R. Howe

Juneau

"Just Say No" in Homeport Vote

To the *Juneau Empire*

September 19, 1988

Dear Editor:

Juneau is a remarkable mix of sophistication and small-town warmth, with a wonderful diversity of people and activities. I believe that if our community becomes a Navy homeport, the character of this place that is so special would alter substantially—and that the changes would be a matter of kind, not just degree. I hope everyone will take the chance to vote for keeping Juneau the Juneau we know, by voting "no" on the homeport question in October. Remember, this is critical to how it will feel to live here in the future. I think many of us like to live here because it is not big and bustling. So let's "just say no" to changing it so much.

Sincerely,

Larri Irene Spengler

Juneau

The Morality of Homeporting

To the *Juneau Empire*

September 20, 1988

Dear Editor:

Homeporting is a moral issue, not just a matter of economics. My previous letter on homeporting raised a profound moral problem for us to consider as a community—that homeporting as economic development was morally wrong for us if our reasons were for making monetary profits. It is wrong to willingly want to make personal monetary profits from war or the preparation for war. As this seemed to be the primary motive for supporting the homeport option—to make money for the community—then homeporting was morally wrong for us.

I raise the issue again because last Friday, the Juneau Economic Development Council published in the Empire a "Summary of Findings" to inform the community about homeporting impacts. The summary stated that homeporting might add 440 to 570 jobs to the local economy, generate $9 to 11 million in payroll annually, and increase revenues by $1.7 to 2.4 million. How does this information affect our moral judgment about homeporting? If the information makes us feel more positive about homeporting, we should be careful. We should stop and think more deeply. Thinking in terms of personal monetary profits moves us down a morally dangerous path.

This is why. Morally, war or the preparation for war should always be a cost to us personally, and a cost to us as a community. Always. We should always experience it as a heavy burden on all of us, emotionally, socially, economically, and spiritually. There is nothing joyful about war or the preparation for war. Modern military preparedness is a sad reality. A sad burden. Why should we experience it this way? Because only then is there the hope that we will work to limit its use. Our Judeo-Christian tradition insists that we feel this way. If we don't feel it, we must introspect and ask ourselves, "why not?"

It is a morally dangerous state of affairs that many of us today no longer experience war or the preparation for war as a sad, burdensome cost. It is even more dangerous that some communities actually come to perceive it as personal monetary profit, like a business. Then, military decisions become confused. We base them on economic information instead of moral or strategic information. Unfortunately, the Development Council's summary sheet does just that: it implies that it is right and proper to make decisions about homeporting based on economic information. We should resist this way of choosing. It is dehumanizing and morally dangerous.

At the last assembly meeting, Mayor Ernie Polley is reported by the Empire to have said he respected this "philosophical" position, but held another one. What is that other moral position? How is it morally good (or morally neutral) for a community to willingly desire to make personal monetary profits from war or the preparation for war? None of the traditional Judeo-Christian religious positions toward war allows for this as moral behavior, to my knowledge. If there is some other moral code to guide us in these matters, it needs to be stated.

Homeporting as economic development in Juneau is not moral. It is wrong for us. We should not support it. We must vote against it on the upcoming ballot.
Sincerely,
Robert J. Wolfe
Juneau

Navy Would Change Structure of Community

To the *Juneau Empire*

September 22, 1988

Dear Editor:

There will be a major change if homeporting happens in Juneau: how decisions will be made in the community. Currently, decisions in Juneau are made out in the open, using public information, with public involvement, through elected officials. If you like this open democratic process, you should be concerned about home-porting. With a two frigate navy and an additional structure of 1,000 to 1,300 Navy personnel, the military will become a major decision-maker in the community. The military's process for making decisions is very different. It is hierarchical, it is closed, and it is not democratic.

What decisions are likely to be made by the Navy if it becomes a major player in Juneau? It is hard to tell at this point. But three likely ones would be determining sites of facilities, locations of operating areas, and restrictions on access to these lands and waters. One big fear is that areas with current recreational, scenic, and biological values will be lost. I intend to vote against the homeport option.

Sincerely,

Stephanie Loris

Auke Bay

Another Vote against Homeport

To the *Juneau Empire*

September 22, 1988

Dear Editor:

After reading the McDowell Group report, I can assure the assembly that I have more than enough information to vote NO to any further spending on studies. Also, from personal experience, I can assure the assembly that I would vote NO to having Juneau selected as a Navy homeport. I spent 12 years of my life in a navy homeport city, 5 years in an army base city, and 3 years in an air force base town. I moved to Juneau partly because I felt it was ONE place that would not be con-sumed and radically changed by the military. Supporting the military has nothing to do with choosing Juneau as a homeport. This is not a strategic area. Having the Navy in Juneau would neither enhance our lives nor be beneficial to the military. I prefer that our energy and resources be used to maintain a community rather than maintain an arsenal.

Sincerely,

Theresa Scott
Douglas

As September progressed, I was puzzled. The *Juneau Empire* favored the home-port. Yet the paper continued to publish anti-homeport letters, all from the cadre of regular readers at the Orpheum. I knew of none turned down. As puzzling, so far the debate was lopsided. Nobody had submitted a pro-homeport letter. What was happening? Did the assembly and civic developers who favored the homeport represent anyone in town? The political tide showed signs of change. A political forum the week following these letters' publication found all the candidates for municipal offices mum on the homeport. Not publicly opposed. Simply mum. All except Rosie Peterson, a local firebrand, who was running unopposed in her assembly district:

Homeport Issue Gets Cool Response from Candidates

The idea of a Navy homeport based in Juneau earned little support Monday night from the candidates running for mayor and assembly. At a forum sponsored by several environmental groups, the candidates raised repeated questions about the impact of a Navy base on the community. "I don't want my little town to be a frigate town," said Rosie Peterson, who is running unopposed for a District 1 seat on the Juneau City-Borough Assembly. Peterson has said she'll vote against an upcoming ballot proposition that will ask if Juneau residents want to continue collecting information about the impacts of a homeport, or if they want to stop the homeport push right now. Aside from Peterson, the other candidates have been cautious in their statements about the homeport.

—Article by Bruce Scandling, *Juneau Empire*, September 27, 1988

Perhaps sensing tidal shifts, that same day the managing editor of the *Juneau Empire* released the paper's second editorial supporting the homeport, the vote a week away. The managing editor directly confronted the moral question. The paper disagreed. The military should be considered a peaceful profession:

"Yes" Vote Keeps Our Options Open

Tuesday's vote on the homeport proposition is little more than a popularity poll on the U.S. Navy, yet advocates and detractors are trying to put their own "spins" on what the issue means to the Capital City. One factor that is crucial to the Navy in choosing a new homeport is whether a community wants it. The question will be answered Tuesday. During the course of public discussion on a homeport, a lot has been said about the Navy in particular and the military in general. Much of it has been less than flattering, unfairly generalizing about the people who serve their nation in uniform. Other discussion has centered on the military as only "preparing for war" and urging that Juneau have no part of it.

We respectfully disagree with both positions. Juneau has had a long and quite cordial relationship with men and women in uniform, in the form of the U.S. Coast Guard, whose district headquarters are in the Capital City. While the Coast Guard and Navy are not identical in their missions or personnel, they are similar in many ways. During its time here, the Coast Guard has demonstrated itself to be a good neighbor—one of the best. Other Alaskan communities have had similar experiences with the military. The thousands of men and women stationed at Elmendorf Air Force Base and Fort Richardson in Anchorage and at Eielson Air Force Base and Fort Wainwright near Fairbanks have demonstrated that the military is in fact the sort of neighbor any community would be proud to have.

The statement that the military is only "preparing for war" is especially troubling. Certainly, the military is the instrument our nation's leaders turn to when they fail, but the main mission of the military is peace. "Peace is our Profession" is the sign posted at the entrance of most Air Force bases. Indeed, the deterrence provided by all branches of the military has maintained a stable peace among the super powers for decades. As long as that military balance is maintained, we can expect that peace to be maintained as well. It is important that Juneau as a community have a say in its future. That is exactly what this proposition provides in regard to a Navy homeport here.

As we go to vote our feelings on a homeport, however, we must make sure we are being fair to the Navy, the community and to ourselves. We must make sure our feelings are based on a fair reading of the available facts and not overly broad statements and theories. We believe the facts at hand and the experiences of other Alaskan communities dictate a "yes" vote on Proposition 5 on the homeport. It will keep our options open, and it will allow us to continue to seek facts about the possibility of a homeport in Juneau's future.

> Managing editor of the *Juneau Empire*, editorial, *Juneau Empire*,
> September 27, 1988

The October 4 election neared, the day for voting. In the ensuing days, the *Juneau Empire* released a backlog of letters on the homeport. The very next day, it printed two particular letters, spreading dread among the Orpheum crowd:

Homeports and the "Sleaze Factor"

To the *Juneau Empire*
September 28, 1988
Dear Editor:

As both a Navy veteran and an 11-year resident of Juneau, I have been observing the current discussion over homeporting two naval vessels here. In all of the glib assurances and purported benefits of such an action, there is one aspect that I haven't heard addressed. Will the City and Borough of Juneau-Douglas deal with the potential sleaze factor before or after the fact?

Ask any veteran, especially ex-sailors and ex-marines, what homeports are like. In fact I would urge a delegation of homeport proponents to go south and visit a few of them before continuing their campaign. Homeports were the number one factor in my decision not to make the military a career. Granted, the ports I was stationed in (Long Beach, California; Norfolk, Virginia; Pensacola, Florida) were all large and were used by entire fleets. Therefore all we're talking about here is a matter of degree. But I honestly feel that even a half mile of the type of establishments that flock around main gates of military installations anywhere in the United States would not be of benefit to this town.

Even if they did generate additional revenue, this type of entrepreneurship would only cheapen the social ambiance of our beautiful capital here in Southeast Alaska. Do not misunderstand. I am not anti-military. I am not worried about what the Navy would do to Juneau, I am worried about what Juneau would do to Juneau.
Very sincerely,
Stoney Compton
Juneau

Homeport Would Inundate Juneau

To the *Juneau Empire*
September 28, 1988
Dear Editor:

I'm writing to express my concern about the homeporting issue. I'm 36 years old, I've lived in four major cities in the U.S., I've been in the military, and I know the kind of insanity (drugs, violence, etc.) that accompanies a military installation. I've searched for 20 years to find a place where people care about the quality of their lives and the place that they live, and I've found that in Juneau. Perhaps if Juneau was a larger city it could absorb a large naval population without sacrificing its heart, but I don't believe it's big enough to do so. There must be better, more holistic ways to financially support our community.

Sincerely,

Gary L. Scott

Juneau

Members of The Reading quickly convened. We knew Gary Scott. He attended some of the Readings. His letter mentioned drugs and violence near military installations. But this was mild compared to Stoney Compton's letter. The paper had titled it "Homeports and the 'Sleaze Factor.'" Who was Stoney Compton? In our group, no one knew. He had not attended any of the Readings. His letter came from outside the group. With just days before the vote, we braced ourselves for backlash. Disparaging servicemen was political suicide in America.

On Friday, September 30, five days before the vote, the *Juneau Empire* brimmed with homeport items. At a hearing of the Juneau Planning Commission, eleven people testified, all opposed to the homeport, reported the paper. On the letters page, the paper published what was to become the single pro-homeport letter from the public. They also printed a rant I submitted about morality and nuclear targets:

Vote "Yes" On Homeport Issue

To the *Juneau Empire*

September 30, 1988

Dear Editor:

We do need someone to support our economy since we will all at some time sell our property and I am sure yours is worth top dollar and so is mine. If we restrict access to the community to protect our piece of the environment, who will we sell to? Had I and others 30 years ago adopted such a policy to protect the parts of our environment that has since been forever changed, how many of you would be here? I intend to vote for the Navy homeport.

Yours,

Albert Shaw

Juneau

Homeports and Military Targets

To the *Juneau Empire*

September 30, 1988

Dear Editor:

Are communities which accept Navy homeports military targets? The answer to this question, according to the Juneau Economic Development Council, is "yes, Navy homeports are military targets." The Navy agrees. According to Rear Adm. Eugene J. Carroll Jr., in all likelihood the Soviet Union will assign strategic nuclear warheads to each new Navy homeport. As we know, strategically the U.S. and the Soviet Union are moving toward the concept and capability of "limited nuclear exchanges." That is, the trend is toward nuclear strategies which target only the nuclear forces and installations of its adversary. Under these new strategies, military targets, like Navy installations, would be hit in a first surgical strike or in immediate defensive retaliation.

Given these trends, should military targets like Navy installations be located in civilian population centers unless there are compelling reasons to do so? For it means tens of thousands of non-combatants become victims as a side-effect of a direct hit on the installation. Morally, the answer to this question is "no." Catholic and mainline Protestant churches hold a central moral position about war and its preparation: that war must be engaged in ways that protect the lives of innocent non-combatants. When preparing for war, plans must be made which limit the loss of non-combatant lives when war is conducted. This tenet about protecting the lives of innocent non-combatants has been central to church doctrine and to historic American moral views about war.

Because of these moral problems, there must be very compelling reasons to locate a military target in a population center like Juneau for it to be morally justified. In Juneau's case, so far there are no compelling reasons, only that home-porting may bring some jobs and some revenue to Juneau. Jeopardizing the lives of a large non-combatant population principally for economic reasons is morally unsupportable.

Sincerely,

Robert J. Wolfe

Juneau

A political advertisement filled an entire page. Volunteers had gathered 353 signatures. Volunteers considered one signature in particular to be a coup, placing it at the top of the list of names, that of Bishop Michael Kenney, head of the archdiocese of Southeast Alaska, beloved by parishioners:

> Plain and simple . . . we don't want a Navy "homeport" in Juneau. Vote "No" October 4 on the Homeport Proposition. Accompanied by signatures of 353 residents.
> Paid for by Juneau Citizens Against Homeporting, John Howe, Chair
> —Full-page political advertisement, *Juneau Empire*, September 30, 1988

And then there was this final letter:

Juneau Voters Face Key Choices October 4

To the *Juneau Empire*
September 30, 1988
Dear Editor:

I am writing to urge Juneauites to vote in the October 4 municipal elections. This election, more than most, has the potential to shape our town for years to come. For all of us who feel frustrated by our lack of power to influence the course of the government and the economy, this is our chance to go out and do something that will count.
Sincerely,
Bart Wilson
Juneau

The letter exhorted everyone to get out to vote. They proved the final words from the public. Nothing ran Saturday. There was no Sunday *Empire*.

On Monday, the day before the election, the managing editor of the *Juneau Empire* fired the last salvo in the homeport debate. It was the third and final editorial on the homeport. The Orpheum crowd groaned. The managing editor was outraged by the so-called Sleaze Factor. How dare anti-homeporters impugn the integrity of servicemen? The editorial demanded an apology from those "running loose" in town:

An Apology Due to the Military

The gentleman at the other end of the phone line was upset, and rightly so. The references to the "sleaze factor" by those opposed to a Navy homeport in Juneau made it sound as though everyone in uniform was a lower class of human being. As a career Coast Guard officer, he felt he and his colleagues stationed in Juneau are being unfairly criticized and not wanted. "Tell them the news—there are already 200 sailors in Juneau," he said. "If the town doesn't want us or any other sailors then maybe we should pull out."

It is true that in their arguments against a homeport, opponents have managed to lump all the uniformed services into a single, low-class group that somehow will bring with them all the evils and ills of society. In the process of making their dubious arguments, they have managed to soil the good reputation of those in Juneau who serve in the Coast Guard and the National Guard. It is more than a little ironic to hear these unfounded, broadside attacks on the military after watching this city's leaders beg and cry when the Cutter *Planetree* was transferred out and the Coast Guard reorganization cost the area jobs.

We believe an apology is due those men and women in uniform. We know them as friends, neighbors and good citizens and we're not willing to stand by as some overly strident homeport opponents paint them as somehow unworthy of living in Juneau. The fact of the matter is, if we had our choice we would take the military over some of the other allegedly "better" people running loose in this town.

> Managing editor of the *Juneau Empire*, editorial, *Juneau Empire*, October 3, 1988

The editor had administered the poison pill, leaving no time for antidotes.

The *Juneau Empire* was not a morning paper. It hit stands the afternoon of the fourth. The lead article covered the municipal election, in progress, and its "nasty" weather. Of course, Juneau's used to nasty weather:

Today's the Day for the Local Voters

Municipal election outcome hinges on today's balloting. Patty Ann Polley, Juneau's municipal clerk, is predicting a higher-than-average turnout for today's election, in which voters will pick a new mayor, fill seats on the assembly and school board, and decide the fate of five ballot propositions. "I do think the weather's affecting people, it's rather nasty out there today," said Polley. The polls close at 8 pm. Centennial Hall is hosting an election night event beginning about 9 pm, said hall manager Bruce Kruger. The public is invited to watch the results come in, he said.

> —Article by Bruce Scandling, *Juneau Empire*, October 4, 1988

I didn't know they had post-election parties at Centennial Hall. I strolled downtown in the nasty weather and joined the festivities. We stood around, ate munchies, and talked, watching the numbers drift in by precinct. Voters had turned out in large numbers. The new mayor, soon to be elected, was working the crowd. He found me out and warmly pumped my hand, grinning from ear to ear. "I think he's thanking us," said someone in my ear. "Huh?" I mumbled. "He may have won the mayor's race because of the higher turnout." "Huh?" I mumbled again. "Because of the homeport, stupid!"

The *Juneau Empire* published the unofficial election results the next day, followed by a *c'est la vie* editorial:

Voters Back Pool, Sink Homeport, Strong Mayor

Voters have apparently torpedoed a push by some local officials to lure a Navy homeport to Juneau. With all precincts reporting in Tuesday's municipal election, 53 percent of Juneau voters said they want to stop any effort to try to attract a Navy base. In all, 3,341 people voted against the homeport, while 2,949, or 46 percent, said they wanted more information before making a final decision. About 700 ballots are still to be counted, but they are not expected to change the results of any of the races.

Of five ballot propositions that faced voters Tuesday, it was the homeport issue that received the most attention and sparked the most debate. The Navy has said it might base some of its ships in Alaska. Juneau was one of ten Alaska communities being considered, according to the Navy and U.S. Senator Ted Stevens, R-Alaska. As of today, the list is apparently down to nine. Jim Kohler, director of the Juneau Economic Development Council, said he believes the Navy will no longer consider Juneau. He also said efforts by the council to win a homeport will stop. "We know now that the community doesn't want to proceed with it, and that's fine," Kohler said. "I know the council, and I assume the city, will not invest any money in trying to pursue it."

Opponents wrote dozens of letters to the editor, testified at public meetings and waved anti-homeport signs on election day. Rosie Peterson, who ran unopposed on Tuesday for a seat on the assembly, was the only candidate to speak adamantly against the homeport. Most candidates said they supported the advisory vote, if only to get more information. Peterson, however, said she detected clear community opposition early on in the campaign. "They're saying, 'We don't even want to study it,'" she said. "I had people coming up to me on the street that I'd never met before (after a newspaper article mentioned her opposition to the Navy base). They were saying, 'Thanks for speaking out for me on the Navy homeport.' "

—Article, not credited, *Juneau Empire*, October 5, 1988

Congratulations and Condolences

Another municipal election is behind us, and about the only race that didn't have a surprise was that for Juneau City-Borough Assembly District 1, in which candidate Rosie Peterson was unopposed. On the propositions, wide margins were recorded only in favor of the swimming pool bond and against considering switching to a strong mayor government. All the other races were extremely tight. The homeport was a close call, with 52 percent of the voters saying they don't want anything to do with a Navy homeport and 47 percent saying they want to continue to keep informed about it. Whether you agree or disagree with the outcome, that's the way it was on Tuesday. We offer our congratulations to winners of Tuesday's election and our condolences to the losers. Hopefully, these results will make us all winners.

Managing editor of the *Juneau Empire*, editorial, *Juneau Empire*, October 6, 1988

Sunday, I strolled through pouring rain to the Orpheum for The Reading, buying the *Anchorage Daily News* at the corner liquor store. The Orpheum was bustling. Everyone smiled and gave high fives, telling and retelling their roles in the political fray. An old left-winger pontificated, something about momentum and building the organization. I sat in a corner to read. I was feeling that I had had my fill of grassroots politics for a while.

"Hey, congratulations!"

It was the same friend with whom I had sat, frustrated, less than three months before, trying to express coherent moral outrage about homeports.

"Thanks," I said, returning to the paper.

"Hey, let's celebrate! We won!"

"Did we?"

"Yeah! Big time!"

"I don't know. Listen. This is bugging me. Why did we win? Why did people vote the way they voted?"

He thought a second, blankly. Then he smiled and shrugged his shoulders.

"Does it matter?"

Juneau was done with the homeport, as was I. But others fumed about the managing editor's cheap shot the day before elections. Personally, I thought the paper had treated everybody pretty fairly. And it cost nothing. You had to admire America's small-town press. A week later, it even published the pissed-off rejoinder:

Editorial Stance Was "Sleazy"

To the *Juneau Empire*
October 11, 1988
Dear Editor:

The issue of "sleaze factor" was raised in your editorial of October 3 when the Empire chose to lump the Navy and the Coast Guard together. In no letters or conversations to which I have been a part has anyone opposed to the Navy voiced opposition to the Coast Guard in Juneau. I oppose the Navy homeporting in Juneau and I am also concerned about the sleaze to which you allude. But I maintain that it may well be your editorial that is the sleaze, rather than the honest opinions of citizens opposed to Navy homeporting in Juneau.
Sincerely,
Jon Lyman, Vonnie Anderson, Judy Hall Alaback, Bill Glude
Juneau

And the next day, Stoney Compton resurfaced, writing in to clarify his first letter:

"Sleaze" Referred to Civilians, Not Navy

To the *Juneau Empire*
October 12, 1988
Dear Editor:

Your editorial in the October 3 issue demanding an apology to the military has a fundamental problem. I request that you and the career Coast Guard officer go back to my letter and read it carefully again. In point of fact I was not referring to any member of the military when I was talking about a sleaze factor associated with larger military bases. I was talking about the civilian sleaze factor that surrounds military installations. The people who promise our young enlisted people anything just to get their signatures on a promissory note; the people who prey on lonely military personnel in a strange town; the creeps with gimmicks and come-ons who only want to separate the gullible from their money as quickly as possible. It's not what the Navy might do to Juneau that worries me, it's what Juneau might do to Juneau.

The Coast Guard is an overworked and under-paid service that does a tremendous job and for whom I have nothing but respect. The respect also stems from the fact that their main job is to save life, not take it, and they also don't bring nuclear weapons into Southeast Alaska.

Most sincerely,

Stoney Compton

Juneau

At the Orpheum, reading his polite response, we wondered. "Who the heck *is* Stoney Compton?"

The homeport vote didn't stay local. The national press picked up the story, misinterpreted the vote, and forced Alaska's powerful senator to wade in. Alaskans shiver at the mere thought of this senator having to "straighten" things out, deftly yanking federal purse strings:

After the Homeport

Officials Near and Far React to Juneau's Anti-Navy Vote

Juneau's vote against a Navy homeport has prompted reaction far beyond city hall. In an opinion column sent to Alaska newspapers this week, U.S. Senator Ted Stevens, R-Alaska, said national press coverage of the Juneau vote implied the whole state is against a homeport. He cited a *Washington Post* headline that said Alaska, rather than Juneau, voted down the homeport. "Several senators mentioned to me that Alaska had rejected homeporting, and I had to straighten that out," he said Tuesday in a telephone interview from his Washington, D.C. office. Despite his surprise over the outcome, Stevens said he believes it was proper for Juneau residents to vote when they did.

The Navy, meanwhile, already has chosen San Francisco as a preferred site for a battleship group, although it has made no definite plans. News of the Juneau vote was picked up by national wire services and hit the *Los Angeles Times* two days after the election. Staffers for San Francisco Mayor Art Agnos were interested, partly because the mayor is opposed to dedicating city funds to the battleship group. They also had never heard of another city rejecting a homeport.

—Article by Bruce Scandling, *Juneau Empire*, October 12, 1988

"Someone's been calling from San Francisco," the Orpheum scuttlebutt confirmed. And Anchorage. And a couple of other places. They wanted to know, how had Juneau stopped a homeport? "Anybody want to take those calls?" I don't remember any volunteers.

The last homeport letter in the *Juneau Empire* got published ten days post-vote. We didn't know the writer, apparently a neighborly Montanan with a finger to the nation's pulse:

If You Don't Want It, We Do

To the *Juneau Empire*

October 14, 1988

Dear Editor:

As a visitor to the state of Alaska on several occasions, I was surprised to read in the *Washington Post* that the folks in Juneau had voted against playing a part in the defense of our nation. As a resident of the state of Montana, I wish we had some shoreline because I can guarantee you the town would be out to welcome the first ship to pull into port. We in Montana look at bases as an asset, not only from a national security standpoint, but also as an integral part of enriching our communities. In Montana, we have coexisted with one of the legs of the strategic nuclear triad since its inception, and the base that coordinates the Minutemen missiles at Great Falls, Montana is considered an asset by all. All you have to do is read the sign as you enter the main gate that says, "Peace is Our Business." That says it all.

Sincerely,

Cy Jemison

Billings, Montana

Alaska never got a Navy homeport. After the environmental impact studies, the concept sort of fizzled. Enthusiasms waned. Some seaports down south received the Navy's graces, we supposed, isolated in landlocked Juneau reading the Sunday news. The papers didn't say. Crude oil prices rebounded. Another governor held office. Daily news logs flowed across my desk with other bold ideas for Alaska's economy. And four years passed. Then on Valentine's Day I noticed a small article toward the back of our small-town paper. A homeport story:

Hitting Home Ports

Critics Claim They're "Pork"

The investigative arm of Congress said they are expensive and unnecessary. A retired admiral who commanded the Navy's 2nd Fleet says they are the ultimate "pork barrel." But despite withering criticism, five new ports the Navy is building appear likely to survive the current wave of military cuts. The new Navy ports are under construction in Ingleside, Texas; Pascagoula, Mississippi; Mobile, Alabama; Staten Island, New York; and Everett, Washington. "I have followed this for some time, and I've been trying to convince the Navy that it was a dumb idea," said Jack Shanahan, a retired admiral who lives in Daytona Beach, Florida. "It became political, as opposed to strategic or tactical. You couldn't make logical arguments against the home ports because it was going to be a pork-barrel project." The idea in the 1980s was to make it difficult for the Soviet military to attack and cripple the Navy's fighting force. "I don't think I have to explain how ridiculous that is today," Shanahan said.

—Article by Dave Moniz, Knight-Ridder Newspapers reporter, *Juneau Empire*, February 14, 1992

I expect this may be the final word.

8

Icebreakers

Tiny Fish, Jonah, and the Avoidance of a

War over Birds between Californians and

Yup'ik Eskimos

Icebreakers. These are sturdy ships built for breaking passages through icebound waters. Nuclear-powered icebreakers secure winter passage in the Far Northern seas of Russia. To avoid icebreakers, the trans-Alaska oil pipeline carries crude oil overland from Prudhoe Bay on the Beaufort Sea to the relatively ice-free port of Valdez on Prince William Sound. But icebreakers are also something else. At parties or meetings, icebreakers are small things said or done to relax tense situations. Icebreakers represent small beginnings. They are tentative starts toward hoped-for ends. Caught within intractable political stalemates, negotiators sometimes pray for icebreakers, any small, humanizing act to break the grip of cold mistrust.

There's a story about birds that involves icebreakers and blackfish, a small, little-known fish about the size of your hand. The blackfish were icebreakers in a tense and dangerous political standoff. They helped to avert a war over birds. In 1983, the little fish played a part in deescalating a showdown between California bird hunters and the Yup'ik Eskimo of the Bering Sea region of western Alaska.

The peaceful resolution of the bird crisis is a story of human empathy. And rather like the biblical story of the prophet Jonah, we shall see that animals played essential parts. As you may recall, Jonah was far from empathetic. He was only persuaded to go to Nineveh to warn its people of their impending destruction after an immense fish swallowed and regurgitated him upon the sands, a lesson about the futility of fleeing responsibility. But you may not re-call that a lowly worm taught Jonah about compassion for enemies who are spared destruction. Like that mythic great fish and that lowly worm, the humble blackfish helped others resolve a cold political impasse. The small fish helped to shake things loose.

In the language of the central Yup'ik Eskimo, blackfish are called *can'giiq*, or *imangaq* in the Yukon dialect. The Yup'iks also call a village this, Emmonak, a place on the Yukon-Kuskokwim Delta where residents trap the small fish for food. Ichthyologists call them *Dallia pectoralis* and put them in the family of mudminnows, reflecting where they live, or maybe how they taste. They are a remarkable fish. I understand that blackfish are living survivals of Beringia, the lost wind-blown steppe that connected Asia and North America during Earth's last great ice age, the so-called Bering Land Bridge, an immense, flat grass-lands of wooly mammoths, bison, dire wolves, camels, and other Pleistocene megafauna, hunted by hardy, roving human bands for thousands of years. Black-fish lived in the freshwater streams and lakes of Beringia. With global warming about eleven thousand years ago, Earth's ice packs receded, the waters of the North Pacific flooded Beringia to form the Bering Sea, the remaining grass-lands turned to tundra, and the megafauna disappeared. But the tiny blackfish endured. They survived in the small channels and ponds of what was once Beringia, in the wet tundra on either side of Bering Strait, and even in the streams of the few mountain peaks poking out from the Bering Sea like St. Lawrence Island and the Pribilofs.

Shallow tundra ponds offer a harsh life to blackfish. The ponds substan-tially freeze each winter, getting cut off from one another unless muskrats and otters maintain connecting channels. Without water flow, the pond's oxygen becomes depleted. But the blackfish have adapted. Their ability to survive cold, low-oxygen environments is legendary. The entry on *imangaq* in Jacobson's *Yup'ik Eskimo Dictionary* states *cikumang'ermeng imangat anertequt*—"even though frozen, the blackfish are alive." Scientists understandably may be skep-tical, but Yup'iks tell many stories of thawing blocks of ice containing blackfish, reanimating the small creatures.

Blackfish deal with depleted oxygen in freezing ponds in an exceptional way. They regularly swim to the tops of ponds, breaking the surfaces for breaths of air absorbed through their throats, a mudminnow trick. Though ponds regu-larly freeze a couple of feet thick, the small areas where blackfish come up to breathe are kept open by the water currents created by the blackfish's own body, the breathing spot glazed with a thin ice film. Yup'ik fishers carefully probe a pond's surface for where the blackfish breathe, for it is here that hand-carried, cylindrical fish traps may be set, vertically, to catch blackfish as they descend to the bottom. Yup'iks eat fresh winter blackfish in soups. They also feed them to their sled dogs. So blackfish work as tiny icebreakers in their own realms. Through persistent, incremental acts, they hold off winter from their homes, carving out room to live in ice. Perhaps their role as icebreakers in the bird crisis should come as no surprise.

Bird migrations are wondrous. How is it that birds successfully traverse vast distances year after year with such diminutive heads? The largest are the size of tightly-rolled socks, shiny eyes poked pinlike to the sides. I understand what scientists assert—birds successfully navigate the vast distances by memory. Birds remember landmarks, star constellations rotating in the black heavens, and slight realignments of the Earth's electromagnetic fields sensed with intracranial lodestones. This all occurs within the rolled-up sock. As I say, it's wondrous.

Consider the Pacific black brant, a small dark goose weighing somewhat less than four pounds. The brants currently fly a long migration route, about three thousand miles, between the warm waters of Baja California, where most of them now winter, and the cool northern seacoasts of the Bering Sea in Arctic Alaska, where they breed, nest, and rear young during spring and summer. Juveniles travel farther yet to the Arctic slope to molt, near the Prudhoe Bay oil fields. How did these long journeys come about? As we learned from the blackfish, a mere ten thousand years ago in geologic time, during the most recent ice age, the Bering Sea did not exist to visit. The land was a dry steppe inhospitable to marine-loving brants. Clearly, they must have nested elsewhere, perhaps toward the southern edge of the ice sheets in Oregon or Washington.

We can imagine the steps leading to the brants' current migration. As the Pleistocene ice packs receded and the Bering Sea flooded, new bird habitat emerged to the north. As northern and southern climes separated, the yearly flights of the brants probably lengthened. What this takes are a few mavericks, feisty individuals willing to explore emerging postglacial landscapes, and a natural flocking tendency in brants. Successful mavericks become leaders. Bird migrations are mass followings, a trust that someone must know the way. Chicks hatch each spring primed to follow, eagerly imprinting, mimicking, and absorbing landmarks tucked within each tiny head. So ancient games of follow-the-leader have created the flyways of today, a yearly chase re-created over tens of thousands of annual cycles.

There's a small salt bay on the southern edge of the Bering Sea on the Alaska Peninsula called Izembek Lagoon where the brants briefly stop on the flight south during fall. It offers abundant food in the beds of eelgrass. For a couple of weeks the brants feed and feed, refueling their small systems before the next astonishing leg, a nonstop leap of faith across the stormy North Pacific to a merciful landfall in Oregon about fifteen hundred miles to the southeast. Today's brants somehow know they must stop at Izembek Lagoon to fuel up before attempting this treacherous leg. Alaska's entire population of Pacific black brants congregates at this one spot, if you want to count them. Bird biologists call it a critical staging area. It receives protection as a federal refuge. Successful brants that reach Oregon head down the Pacific coast, leapfrogging between coastal bays to the Baja.

The migrations of birds like the Pacific black brant create remarkable living connections. They link our planet, north and south, east and west, season to season. A great many species make such living links—butterflies, sea turtles, salmon, whales. In a decade of public protest against increased globalization, the global linkages long established by living creatures may get overlooked. Of course nature has interconnected the planet far longer than has human trade, for good or for bad. And though they may be unaware, groups of people far distant in geography and culture get connected by animals. It's that way with bird migrations. People become connected along the invisible aerial flyways established by birds.

Such became the case for the Yup'ik Eskimo of western Alaska and a new, emerging group to the south—the Californians. Three geese in particular— black brant, cackling Canada, and white-fronted geese—became feathered ambassadors between them. The Yup'iks had hunted the Arctic-nesting geese for a long time, perhaps for thousands of years. The Californians, arriving with the gold rush of 1849, had begun to hunt them more recently. Each spring, the Yup'iks were reading signs carried by the birds about new happenings to the south. But it was understandable that they had trouble interpreting the tidings. Out of sight, beyond the horizon, a great revolution was underway within a new Golden State.

The Yup'ik Eskimo of the Bering Sea coast in Alaska receive migratory birds in spring with great celebration. They are winged messengers of an awakening promise for a land still asleep beneath the winter's snows. It doesn't matter that the rivers and seas are commonly locked in ice during May—the birds still come. Even though the tundra lies frozen hard beneath their feet, the birds descend from brightening skies. Their loud *luk luk lukking* heralds change, quick change, just ahead. Get ready, they seem to cry out, summer's almost here! The rivers will break and flow free. The winds will blow in fish from the sea in successive waves—smelt, char, herring, Chinook, chum, pinks, and more. The lean is transforming to plenty, empty to full. Disentangle the nets. Patch the boats. Gather driftwood to repair the fish-drying racks. Summer's behind our wings.

During the nineteenth century, many Yup'iks along the coast between the Yukon and Kuskokwim rivers wore bird skins. I'm told that neighboring Yup'ik tribes viewed this as poverty—bird skins! It seemed to them that the lowly coastal fringes of the Yukon-Kuskokwim Delta were too poor to produce the richer furs such as the upland parka squirrel or the woodland beaver or the hides of caribou and highly valued Siberian white reindeer. But I think their assessment was wrong. This was a sign of wealth. There were so many birds along the coast, one could wear them! Every year, one could afford to make a bird skin parka because birds returned in such abundance. They made wonderful garments. A plump Yup'ik baby trussed up in eider skin smiled from a warm, dry, cushioned world. An egg hunter arrayed in feathers resembled some tall, ungainly crane high stepping across the wet tundra.

The ways of hunting birds are preserved in historic photographs and museum collections. Yup'ik bird hunters hurled sealskin bolas from blinds. With spear-throwers, hunters in kayaks launched long bird spears side-hafted with ivory points. Hunters fired blunt-pointed bird arrows from sinew-backed bows. And during the midsummer molt on the wetlands, families herded flocks of flightless ducks into enclosures. Birds were taken by the hundreds, by the thousands. And the birds returned by the hundreds of thousands each year. The bird migrations and the spring and summer hunts continued into the twentieth century, when firearms became standard and cotton cloth traded along global markets replaced bird skins. And the Yup'iks of the Bering Sea coast continued to rejoice in the birds and their messages of hope. In the midwinter ceremonies, as walrus-gut drums pounded, the bird spirits danced with humans in the community centers of the villages. Masks of birds sometimes worn by dancers called their *luk luk luks*. Dance fans rimmed with feathers swished out the rhythms of beating wings. And drummers sang out the gratitude of the Yup'ik people for the unfailing promise of the seasons.

During the late 1970s, when I researched traditional hunting by Yup'iks, I ate my share of spring birds. They were served up in the soups and stews of many village homes of the Bering Sea region. I remember my first spring bird hunt, walking along frozen sloughs with Yup'ik hunters. I was wrapped in a borrowed jacket, a borrowed shotgun strapped to my shoulder, pushing someone else's sledge. I didn't even have a state hunting license. I had no real inclination to hunt, only an interest to be a participant observer of customary and traditional subsistence pursuits. But this anthropological affectation struck the Yup'ik hunters as peculiar. You can't go bird hunting without a gun, they pointed out, and so they had me properly outfitted. As I slogged through icy overflows, slipping on transparent late-spring ice filled with bubbles and dead vegetation, I recall losing all sensation in my feet. It was the rubber boots from an army surplus store in Anchorage. They leaked. I wondered if I would sacrifice my toes to witness a bird hunt.

I observed much that was new to me on that first outing. I was surprised that migrating birds would arrive to breed at a place still covered in deep snow and ice, with few visible signs of green. It was a late spring that year, but the birds were on schedule. And they were busy, searching for food and mates and nesting locations. The birds flew back and forth along the coast following semi-predictable paths, and hunters knew likely places and times to find them. Blinds were constructed from driftwood. The Yup'iks were expert in producing loud, authentic duck calls and geese calls from somewhere near the backs of their throats, vibrating a lump of saliva at the upper rear surface of the tongue. I just sat entranced, listening to the amazing replications. The hunters were happy to entertain me. "Here's one for white-fronted geese," they said. "Here's one for mallards." This time of year, birds could be called down from their paths in the sky. They would circle once or twice around us, looking for the calling birds, before peeling off or getting shot. A bird was taken every third shot, by my count. Though I was cold and stiff, their bodies were warm, soft, and limp within my cupped hands. They had traveled many miles to be there. The hunters took the small bodies and propped them up with twigs as decoys. They were grouped like a resting flock to appeal to the eyes of other birds looking for places to land. The Arctic winds were stiff, the drifts were thigh deep, and the day was long. I was bone tired by the time we approached the village. I saw it several miles ahead, steaming with human life in the Arctic twilight, long before we reached it. I did not lose my toes.

In the pictures from that period, I have a photograph of a Yup'ik child, maybe just four years of age, helping her mother in the kitchen. She is helping to pluck a bird. It looks as if she might be kneading bread dough on a cutting board. But there are little fluffs of down drifting on the air. The child is really too young to be able to do this, for it's hard work to pluck a bird, and the mom is smiling just beyond her. Yup'ik children learn about birds before memory.

I recall a sandhill crane lying on a beat-up wooden table in a kitchen of an elderly Yup'ik couple. It's the size of a large pet, presented to the couple by a young hunter. The old woman is working on it, plucking and prodding and then says, "Ahhhh!" With wonder in her eyes to match the tone of her voice, she pulls out an egg, holding it at arm's length toward me. It's larger than her hand. "Looook," she whispers, drawing the word out with a reverence, as if she held an unexpected, priceless pearl. The next morning, there was hard-boiled crane egg on her table, with dried salmon, seal oil, canned peaches, and tea.

One summer, I found myself on a hunt on a Yukon River slough, looking for seals and beluga whales. During summer, young bearded seals sometimes feed up the freshwater channels many miles from the sea. Beluga whales are encountered more occasionally, chasing fish at the river mouths. As we rounded a bend in a meandering slough, we surprised a raft of molting Canada geese. In a panic, the flightless geese tried to take off, frantically skittering in all directions over the top of the water. The driver abruptly geared down the outboard while a companion made several quick shots before the geese disappeared beneath the overhanging brush along the banks. The hunters were grateful, as this was the only luck after a long day's hunting. We picked up several floating birds. A bit later we passed a second group of swimming geese, but the hunters passed them by. We already have birds, they explained to me. I had hoped to eat fresh geese that night. But at dinner I learned that all the birds had been given away to a relative traveling by skiff to the next village up the coast. Perhaps they had geese that night. We ate beluga given to us by someone else.

There were always new things for me to learn about birds and bird hunting. I was conducting a subsistence survey in the home of a Yup'ik hunter in Alakanuk, a small village along one of the many channels formed by the Yukon River as it enters the Bering Sea. The Yupik name of the village, *Alarneq*, means "an error." I was told that in the old days a kayaker following the sloughs south down the Bering Sea coast was taking a wrong turn if he went that way. I was somewhat surprised by the hunter's answers to the survey, suggesting that he didn't do much fishing or hunting the previous year. I knew his family was a heavy user of wild foods. Eventually, he explained. It was because of his hospitalization and post-op recovery last spring. I settled into my chair to hear the story.

He had been seal hunting during spring near the middle mouth of the Yukon River. Suddenly while hunting, he doubled up with pain in his gut, about here, he pointed to his lower right abdomen. His hunting partners rushed the skiff back to the village. He was quickly evacuated by plane to the Alaska Native Hospital in Anchorage, where an emergency appendectomy was performed. They operated just in time, before the appendix had ruptured. In recovery, the surgeon came to check on him and to satisfy a personal curiosity. The surgeon said they were all astonished at what they had found in his appendix. The hunter paused for dramatic effect. What was that, I asked? Look up there, he indicated, nodding his head toward a small glass jar on a mantel. I took down the jar and poured its contents into my hand. Buckshot, small black lead pellets. The shiny beads were mixed with tiny white bones, more than could fit into my palm without spilling over. It *was* astonishing. And that was just some of it, he said.

One can establish (or confirm) at least three facts from this tale. How the human appendix works. The great number of birds that Yup'iks may eat during the course of a lifetime. And the fact that some people don't chew before swallowing.

Chevak is a Yup'ik village a bit south of Alakanuk, near prime nesting areas for geese and ducks along the Bering Sea coast. At Chevak and nearby Hooper Bay, many hunters are experts about birds and their habits. They have watched birds for a long time. Some experts were observing trends—since their grandfathers' time, fewer and fewer birds were returning each year to nest along the coast. Not just the birds hunted for food like the white-fronted and cackling geese, but also the small birds like the rock sandpiper, longspur, and red phalarope. Though a great many birds left in fall, it seemed that fewer birds were returning each spring, fewer than in the people's memory.

One Yup'ik elder in Chevak explained to me why he thought fewer birds were returning each year to nest. He said the membrane separating the two worlds was getting thicker. The membrane was like a drumhead, like the stretched, translucent walrus skin within the wooden hoop pounded by the singers, reverberating in the winter dances celebrating the animals. You see, a bird gives itself to a hunter to be killed. When the bird is used well and is given respect, its imperishable aspect passes through the membrane to the other world beneath this one. There it stays, waiting to be reborn another spring when the eggs are laid and hatched. This is the cycle of nature. But it seemed to the elder, since the Christian era had arrived in the Bering Sea region, the division between worlds was thickening. It was becoming harder and harder for living beings to pass back and forth. Humans rarely could accomplish it any longer like the shamans of old. It also was becoming harder for birds. "What were we doing in this present era to create these difficulties," wondered the elder? He said as a challenge to me, "What might we do as humans to help the birds?"

In the Golden State far to the south, Californians were flush with the vigor of new statehood in 1850. Great projects were being laid for the settlement of the West—railroads linking the East with the Pacific, massive aqueducts diverting water to cities and farms, and irrigation projects reclaiming agricultural lands in the central valley for feeding everexpanding populations. Americans were heading west. California was exploding. Over the next century, California's population would grow from ninety-two thousand people in 1850 to over ten million in 1950. By 2000, there would be over thirty-three million Californians.

The robust growth of California was unknown in western Alaska. During this historic period, the Yup'iks suffered unimaginable tragedy. Like many other Native American societies, the Yup'iks were devastated by diseases introduced from the south by fur traders, commercial whalers, miners, and missionaries— half were killed by smallpox in 1838, nearly half again lost to measles in 1900 and the influenza pandemic of 1919, and more again during the tuberculosis epidemics of the 1930s and 1940s. Between successive waves of death, the Yup'iks struggled back, regrouping depleted settlements, reasserting traditional subsistence practices that had usually sustained them. Along the Bering Sea, it was not an era of expansion. It was a time of great sorrows.

And what of the birds, the feathered messengers tying Yup'iks with Californians? How were they faring? When the vast wetlands of California's central valley were drained for farming, who counted impacts on migratory birds like the cacklers and white-fronted geese? When the coastal estuaries were dredged and filled to create San Francisco, Los Angeles, San Diego, and other places, who assessed costs to marine geese like the brant, or to shorebirds like the sandpiper and phalarope? Few had cataloged their names, let alone their habits, habitats, or numbers.

There was a great revolution underway in the great state of California. It would take Californians less than a hundred years to remove 95 percent of the state's wetlands. Most of the winter habitat used by the ducks and geese of the Pacific Flyway was gone in a single human lifespan. Only 5 percent would remain by the mid-twentieth century. And the survival of that remaining 5 percent was no sure thing. In fact, it was precarious. For the Yup'iks, themselves struggling to survive, the annual message brought by the migrating birds was this—many departed in fall, fewer and fewer returned in spring. This was the birds' message that a new age was dawning.

The political saga of bird protection in California and the continental United States is a tale of hard struggle by thousands, involving the self-education of a civilized nation about responsibilities toward nature. The coming of the conservationists and the ecological movement in America was much belated. But because of this movement, American society put breaks to the nearly complete destruction of wetland bird habitat in California. It took public action, applied science, hardball politics, and hundreds of millions of dollars. Laws to prevent unregulated bird hunting for sport and sale were hammered out, international bird treaties between the United States and Canada in 1916 and with Mexico in 1936. A system of parks and refuges was established to protect natural lands, many managed for winter bird habitat. Small patches of wetlands were preserved by conservationists and sport hunters to help save the remaining 5 percent. And so, the tides of destruction began to turn.

I examined my first live blackfish in a kitchen of a modest village home. It was resting in a few inches of water within a soup pot on the kitchen table. "It's a pet," the householder smiled. "What do you feed it?" I asked. "Things we eat," she said. "It keeps me company." I observed the small fish up close. Thin, about seven inches long, a brownish green, it was largely a flattish head and great, fanlike fins, two toward the front, almost like lobed flippers slowly moving side to side, and two large fins toward the rear, top and bottom. It had large, amphibious eyes. To me, it looked decidedly prehistoric, something as likely to crawl out of the pot as stay in. Sitting in a few inches of water with no gravel, no plants, no aerator, no nothing, it looked rather deprived. "It's grown a lot," she said. I could see this was a species used to hardship, used to long waits in confined spaces with little water, designed for resting in moist, mossy tundra gulping air, waiting for a pond to refill. This little fish was a survivor.

Given history and the natural paths flown by birds, it was inevitable that the ecological conflicts in California would embrace Alaska. The town of Barrow, perched on the northernmost spit of the continental United States, was dragged into the fray in 1961. That summer a game warden arrested a local hunter, an Inupiat Eskimo, for killing an eider. The 1916 bird treaty with Canada, the hallmark convention halting the devastating overharvest of birds in North America, clearly prohibited bird hunting during spring and summer. This included Barrow, Alaska. Of course, the legal seasons were not designed for (or by) the Inupiat, but for regulating sport hunters. The Inupiat were incredulous—how can we legally hunt to eat? The birds are gone during the open season. The law was unreasonable. Its enforcement threatened the survival of the Inupiat as hunting peoples. The next day, over a hundred Inupiat hunters arrived at the game warden's office, each carrying a duck. Arrest us too, they insisted. The civil disobedience was dubbed the Barrow Duck-In.

The federal government retreated, partially, beginning decades of tense uncertainty in the North. Were duck hunters criminals? Or were they responsible citizens feeding villages? The government danced around it. Federal enforcement generally ignored eider infractions in places like Barrow, a so-called nonenforcement policy, informally referenced in agency memos, but unclear and dubiously legal. To Alaska Native leaders, federal agents promised to work toward amending bird treaties to recognize traditional bird hunts in Alaska. However, such amendments proved slow going. They frequently stalled within a tangle of interests in the halls of power. It was a long, difficult wait. Alaska Natives nervously hid birds when public safety officers strode through town. Their badges were veiled threats of what could be done, but might not, though no one was sure, a modern-day bogey man village moms used with fussy toddlers—"Quiet, look out, or that *kass'aq* will hear you." Biologists established test plots in Alaska's new wildlife refuges, surprising Yup'ik women collecting eggs. "Please leave our test plots alone," the biologists asked frightened women. Bird researchers coined a new term, *passive enforcement,* as they erected observation towers in nesting areas—if we're watching, maybe they won't hunt or gather. *Nonenforcement*—it was an ugly era of intimidation, conspiratorial deceptions, and gnawing distrust.

Open conflict over birds nearly erupted in 1983. That year California sports hunter associations threatened a lawsuit challenging the nonenforcement policy. The sportsmen wanted the courts to order the federal government to do its job, that is, enforce the ban on spring and summer bird hunting. The threat sucked the Yup'iks of the Yukon-Kuskokwim Delta into the bird conflict. The geese to be named in the lawsuit nested on Yup'ik lands—white-fronted geese, cackling Canada geese, and Pacific black brants. The numbers of these Arctic-nesting geese had fallen so low in California that sport bags and seasons were nearly gone. What else could be done, reasoned the sport hunters? We can't manufacture habitat. California's birds are produced elsewhere. Sportsmen cast an eye northward and saw a fact—the Yup'iks were illegally hunting. And California sport hunters felt bled enough. The time was ripe for court action. The northern harvest must be restricted, by court order if necessary, to restore birds to California. By happenstance it seems, that year of the looming suit, formal steps for amending the Canadian treaty were filed by the federal government. Bird management policy was in a tug-of-war, torn in two directions.

As an anthropologist employed by the Alaska Department of Fish and Game, I watched events unfold in Alaska. Disturbing images were conjured up in my department's meetings, should the litigants prevail. Airborne troopers, ordered to enforce, would fly into Alaska's wetlands. Buzzed by planes, angry hunters might raise their gun sights. People would fall victims to reckless efforts to enforce flawed treaties. Court orders might escalate a treaty stalemate into a modern "Indian War," a war over birds. "So be it," proclaimed some hard-nosed biologists, "if that's what it takes to protect the geese." "Not on my watch," shouted others, pounding tables and skipping across the floor in gorillalike power displays.

Meetings. "There have to be meetings," reasoned federal and state bureaucrats in the sessions I attended. Such meetings might buy time to forestall the impending disaster. Put the Yup'ik hunters and California sportsmen in the same rooms, face to face, talking and exchanging information. Such a last-ditch effort might convince the hunters to do something to stop the escalation. Some meeting of the minds might defuse this ticking time bomb.

That winter of 1983–84 blew in fast and stormy. Federal and state agencies rushed together four convocations—three in Alaska at Bethel, Chevak, and Hooper Bay, and one in California at the Sacramento National Wildlife Refuge. Hunters representing Yup'ik interests flew in by small plane, organized into a Waterfowl Conservation Committee by Nunam Kitlutsisti, Protectors of the Land. It was the grassroots environmental arm for the Association of Village Council Presidents, the consortium of tribal governments on the Yukon-Kuskokwim Delta. Delegates drawn from various California interests flew in from the south—the California Waterfowlers' Association, Waterfowl Habitat Owners' Alliance, California Department of Fish and Game, the Pacific Flyway Council, and the Audubon Society. The U.S. Fish and Wildlife Service and the Alaska Department of Fish and Game spearheaded the sessions. Public walk-ins, bird researchers, and agency staff hugged side seats in the showdown.

It's hard to imagine less auspicious circumstances. The government was convening the aggrieved and the threatened. In the opening greetings, federal agents conveyed the threat—unless hunters at these meetings did something, the police would act, so let's cooperate. A bludgeoning from science followed this odd exhortation, biologists presenting hours of maps and graphs and data tables about black brants, white-fronted geese, and cacklers, their distributions, numbers, nest densities, clutch sizes, and so on. "We're not here to debate numbers," flatly declared federal representatives. But to be slowly buried beneath them. Translators halted every scientific point to reconvey the messages back and forth between English and Yup'ik speakers, so all might understand. Harsh coffee flowed from huge canisters. Enthusiasm wore low.

Then the gatherings awoke to incendiary allegations, offhand asides, impromptu floor speeches, assertions of belief, blatant accusations. Fingers pointed every direction. Someone blamed spring hunting for the bird declines. No, excessive fall hunting, someone retorted. Someone blamed egging. No, biological field camps disturbed nesting areas. Hunting by commercial herring fishermen. Habitat loss in California. Pesticides. Coastal floods. Blame enough, many times over.

Then came the conciliatory pleas for self-restraint, for self-imposed cooperative solutions. The Yup'iks should voluntarily restrict their hunting, insisted the federal and state agents. Californians already had. Such a demonstration by Yup'iks, if verified by monitors, might mollify California sportsmen, forestalling a suit. It might help the birds recover.

Negotiations began. The Yup'iks' Waterfowl Conservation Committee discussed moratoriums, season closures, habitat protection, population goals, and disturbance. From the onset, the Yup'iks negotiated—they cared about birds. But the moods of the moment were dark and the statements from the floor hardedged. "I was trained from the ancestors to live from the land, to go where you want to go, with the freedom to gather where you want." "Every time we talk, it seems a different species is added to the list." "The declines have occurred, but I see nothing showing why the declines have occurred." "I'm uncomfortable for being blamed for the decline." "These are serious accusations that we've done nothing for the birds." "The birds double themselves when they leave." "We hate to be just bird hatcheries up here for the sports hunters." There was little reason to hope that the springtime promise of legal wrath would be unmade, or repented. War was brewing. The storm clouds gathered.

Jonah the prophetic book seethes with the promise of wrath for Nineveh, their final apocalypse. The great fish spews Jonah upon the Mediterranean shore, launching God's judgment of doom. Overpowered by the ocean storm, cowed by his near death and resurrection within the fish, Jonah reluctantly relents to go to the Assyrians as the emissary of death. At Nineveh, Jonah preaches destruction. His words fire hot and unequivocal. In forty days, God will destroy everyone, everything! But in a strange twist of events, for some reason, the Assyrians of the great city of Nineveh listen. They accept the threats from the angry foreigner. They respond. The common people commit en masse to change. Nineveh's king, observing the example set by his people, follows suit, fasting and praying in sackcloth. And in the strangest twist of fate, observing these honest displays of good intent, God repents his anger. God turns the destruction aside. The judgment of doom lifts. Nineveh is spared. And the prophet Jonah? He's completely disgusted. He skulks angrily near the outskirts of Nineveh. He wants to die, disgusted by the compassion and second chances given his enemy.

What turns humans away from war, to reject it as a solution? Geopoliticians are naïve to credit displays of strength and tough, self-interested negotiations. Those things lead to the very brink of war, not away. In the bird crisis, it wasn't bluster that moved the standoff away from a looming disaster. Nor was it data. The piles of paper charts and tables displayed by science did not cause good will. The Yup'iks already knew the troubles of birds. Before the biologists' test plots and aerial transit surveys and peer-reviewed reports, the Yup'iks knew birds, from experience, year after year. And they cared. As did Californians. A tedium of science broke nothing loose. Nor was it one side accepting the finger of blame. As hunting peoples, Yup'iks understand the great effects of people on animals. Disturbance drives away. Waste destroys. Destruction of habitat limits. Pollution kills. California hunters know this too. And neither side concurred about causes. No, what helped to break the grip of cold mistrust, to affirm and eventually cement good will, were quite different things.

The third meeting was held in the great central valley of California. The Yup'ik delegates flew in to attend. For most, it was the first time they had seen the winter residence of the birds they hunted every spring and summer. The second day was planned for field trips, to give chances for guests to observe the operations of the refuge and nearby hunting clubs. Yup'iks and Californians were paired up. Early that morning, several pairs left to hunt birds, some to public lands, others to private reserves of the clubs.

Some of us received tours of the refuge and its surroundings. The central valley where the refuge was set was impressively flat and open, much like the Yukon-Kuskokwim Delta. It seemed devoid of people, its population removed to urban centers with mechanized agriculture. But even to untrained eyes it was easy to see, unlike western Alaska, the land was developed for planting. The area north of Sacramento was a vast region groomed and managed for cultivation at the grandest industrial scale. Empty of people, but fully developed.

The Sacramento National Wildlife Refuge also was developed, laid out with dikes and squared plots, planted with grains, flooded and drained on careful schedules. The wildlife refuge was nature managed as a farm, a manicured winter range designed for birds. Hunting was also managed, blocks opened and closed by time, day, and season. Our refuge guide joked that the birds learned the schedules to avoid hunters. On this 5 percent of remaining wetlands nature was blended with aviculture, unlike anything seen in western Alaska. It was wondrous. Professionals were paid to look after birds. During their winter's stay the birds were neither fully wild nor fully domesticated. In California, they lived closely associated with people in a contrived codependency. I wondered, how must the birds feel when they arrive in western Alaska after the spring migration, where there are no straight-line dikes and no planted fields to eat and nothing is planned except by nature? Which of these two places now feels more like home?

The Yup'ik delegates also had seen an eyeful, returning from the morning hunts. Before the afternoon sessions began, there was wonder in the comments shared among themselves. What they had witnessed was unlike anything back home. Reams of paperwork were required to hunt. Giant bird decoys, cutout silhouettes of geese taller than hunters, were erected to attract birds. Clever dogs retrieved ducks on command.

"We sat in a blind," described one hunter, "a few feet from another blind. It also had hunters. They were just a few feet down from more hunters. It was shoulder-to-shoulder hunters, all the way down. There was no room."

Another hunter described his morning. "There were ducks in front of us, lots of ducks. Everyone looked at their watches. Everyone waited, looking at the swimming ducks, looking at the watches. Then suddenly, boom! All the guns fired at once, like a war. Then we're done. No more ducks."

Another hunter related facts learned from his partner. "The birds are sick, packed too close. They hire people to patrol each morning, just to pick up dead floating ducks, dead from disease. They pick it up so it doesn't spread."

A Yup'ik delegate arrived late, somewhat breathless. "He shot his brother!" he announced. "Just down from us. He accidentally shot his brother!"

I saw heads shaking. I imagined the way things were back home, the open spaces, the healthy birds, and the free movements of birds and hunters. I heard someone murmur what many of the Yup'iks were thinking—"Poor Californians."

Chevak hosted a pivotal meeting in the commons of its high school, blasted by winter storms. The first day had been long and rough, filled with turgid data, implied threats, and accusations. It was not going too well. Joe Friday, the eldest man in Chevak, stood up to make a speech, translated from the Yup'ik. "He hopes there will be cooperation in this meeting, because if we don't go in that direction, then nothing will get accomplished," summarized the translator. Also, there was an invitation. The Chevak dance group would perform for the guests that night. Dancing had been revitalized after years of inactivity in Chevak, especially because of Joe Friday. The community had a potluck prepared in the school's cafeteria, ready to be eaten, to be followed by dancing.

We found that the community of Chevak had laid a feast for the visitors. On folding head-tables sat rows and rows of serving trays and pots, mounded with food. All the delegates eagerly lined up, famished after a long, contentious day. It was then I noticed an odd thing happening. The Yup'ik delegates were piling their plates high with food, saying things like, "Here's my favorite." "This is good." "I haven't had this in a long time." Like the French, Yup'iks are connoisseurs of gourmet food. The foods of western Alaska must count among the world's great cuisines. For the Yup'ik guests, this was a sumptuous feast. But the non-Native delegates from California and Anchorage were looking hopelessly at the table. Their plates were nearly empty. They were searching for something edible. The famished were unable to eat.

I remember just some of the spread that night. There were platters piled high with half-dried herring, a specialty at Chevak. The herring were still braided in beach-grass strands, glistening with seal oil, just removed from a seal poke. Yup'ik guests grabbed herring with gusto and twisted, leaving the head in the braid and the rest for the plate. There was dried seal meat, black and dense as coal, hacked through with sharp knives like licorice. There were herring eggs on kelp, bursting from a sack, gathered last spring from the beaches. There were stews of seal meat, with rice and onions. There were mounds of dried tomcod, hard flesh shriveled tight along bony rib cages, tiny-toothed, wraithlike mouths gaping wide. "I'm allergic with those," a Yup'ik delegate remarked to me while dishing up at the table, "but I love them; so be careful." There was beluga whale, large, thick white slices of blubber with an attached gray skin, like thick meringue pie. There was dried pink salmon. In large serving bowls was *akutaq* made of whipped Crisco, seal oil, berries, and northern pike. I think there was air-dried caribou and some walrus dish, but my memory begins to fail.

The non-Native guests peered this way and that, looking both hopeful and helpless at the same time. On their plates were dinner rolls, margarine, and jello, with little bits of this and that unknown item placed carefully to the edges. Mostly, their plates were showing white. One California delegate was watching a Yup'ik delegate ladling something like stew from a huge, black pot. "What's that?" I overheard him ask. "Blackfish stew!" he was told with gusto, "My favorite!" Left alone with the ladle, I watched the Californian dip into stew and lift out a portion. There was a horror on his face. In the ladle lay a whole, boiled blackfish. The tiny fish was puffed up tight inside its skin, a short thick black balloon nearly bursting. Its two large amphibious eyes bulged out on either side like white tumors. "What the hell is that!" he exclaimed to me. "A blackfish," I said. He looked at me as if to say, is this some poor joke? He carefully replaced the ladle.

The Yup'ik dances went on for hours. It was an astonishing performance on the high school stage. Young, beautiful teenagers, moving through elaborately choreographed stories to the deafening, pounded rhythms of singing men with drums. The girls, in headdresses of furs, feet planted hard to the floor, wildly moved dance fans rimmed with feathers. Boys in parkas, with hand masks, knelt on the floor before them. They danced to celebrate the first boardwalk built above the tundra in Chevak, mimicking the sprightly step of happy walkers. They danced commemorating the first barge of summer, coming into town with supplies after the sea ice recedes. They danced to celebrate the geese flying in from the south, protecting eggs from foxes, calling out to their life mates. On and on, set after set, song after song, they danced, ensnared by the demands of the drummers, until sweating and panting, they leaned like weary athletes after a championship series.

That night about midnight, I roused from early sleep from my bag on the floor. There were lights and low voices in the high school kitchen. I went over to see. There in the kitchen were delegates from California and Anchorage, heads inside the school's refrigerator. They were starving after the evening's feast, looking for something to eat. "Hey, look at this!" And to smiles a large box of chicken eggs was extracted from the school's icebox. They sat around the kitchen frying up chicken eggs, talking about the day. There was weary self-reflection, no bluster. And that carried over into more subdued and careful speeches the next day, which went much more smoothly than the day before. I heard no one say it, but there seemed to be a growing awareness about life in this part of the world, on the edge of the Bering Sea, with little money and few stores, where feasts came from the land, if they came at all. The way each savored his eggs, sneaked from a refrigerator at midnight, seemed to express it: what a place this is to be living! We'd be eating birds too.

The fourth meeting passed the Hooper Bay agreement. Delegates at a special conference of the Association of Village Council Presidents approved it. Revised later, it evolved into the Yukon-Kuskokwim Delta Goose Management Plan. The agreement contained simple statements of intent between parties to take fewer of the birds in trouble. Joint affirmations of good faith. And it was sufficient. The crisis dissipated into a cooperative program to increase the numbers of geese. For their part, the Yup'iks agreed to stop hunting when nesting began. They would collect no eggs from the troubled geese. For their part, the Californians agreed to further reduce takes of the geese. They pledged to continue their efforts to conserve and protect wetlands for birds in California. Both sides agreed to oppose oil development in sensitive bird areas.

The Yup'ik delegates offered more than this in negotiations. They proposed moratoriums of all hunting of the geese until their numbers increased. The California representatives, a bit shaken by this radical proposal, had to reject it for habitat concerns. Private gun clubs owned half of the remaining California wetlands. Without any chance to hunt white-fronted geese, wetlands might be sold off to agriculture. The Yup'iks yielded. The Yup'ik delegates also proposed curtailing all disturbances in nesting colonies, not only gathering eggs, but disturbances by biological field camp activities as well, including tagging nests and marking eggs. Here the scientists balked, for this radical proposal would mean less data, fewer research dollars, fewer publications, less "passive enforcement." Scientists rejected it, even as a short-term experiment.

God redeems Nineveh. The prophet Jonah sulks alone, brooding in the hot sun, angry about the turn of affairs, angry about the solution. Jonah's callousness piques God. Has Jonah no empathy, no compassion? Has Jonah no sympathy for others different from himself? So God appoints a plant, a climbing gourd, to cover Jonah with cooling shade. Jonah sits briefly comforted. Then appears the lowly worm, appointed by God to eat up the shade. The worm, like the great fish, plays his part. The worm eats, the gourd withers, a hot wind blows, and Jonah sulks miserably again. He's prepped for the question. "Do you miss that plant?" It's rhetorical. Jonah's misery shows all. God finishes the lesson. "You miss a small plant, one you didn't even make; shouldn't I care about the fates of one hundred twenty thousand Assyrians, plus all their animals?" The ancient tale leaves us wondering. Does Jonah ever get it?

For all the effort, the Hooper Bay accord did not stop a lawsuit. Sport hunters filed it a year later, but not Californian hunters—two Alaskan sportsmen associations filed it. Their representatives had not attended the winter meetings of 1983–84. Perhaps if they had, things would have turned out differently. Californian sportsmen refused to join the suit. They stuck to their guns and kept their commitments to the Yup'iks and the goose recovery plan. The suit took years to wend its way through the legal system. When it eventually came to trial and arguments, and the federal judge finally ruled, the court's ruling caught the litigants short. The court affirmed that indeed, spring hunting by Yup'iks was banned under the 1916 international treaty. But the court refused to order any enforcement of the ban. It did not want to disrupt the voluntary goose management efforts underway. The court chose not to forcibly impose a flawed international treaty when grassroots alternatives were working. Good intent and face-to-face cooperation prevailed over the faceless rule of law.

Of course bird numbers and bird distributions constantly change, something well known to the Yup'iks, Californians, and other bird experts. Since the signing of the Hooper Bay agreement, the white-fronted geese and cackling Canada geese of the Pacific Flyway have grown in numbers. Pacific black brant populations have stabilized. Good signs. But I'm told that the brants and cacklers have effectively abandoned California as wintering areas. The brants now primarily winter in the Baja. The cacklers are now choosing southern Oregon to winter. There some farmers view them as pests. For their work to help the brants and cacklers, California hunters have not hunted as many as they might have hoped for. But white-fronted geese populations have increased, and the birds still choose to use California's central valley, offering good hunts for the sportsmen. On the Yukon-Kuskokwim Delta, parties have renewed the goose plan annually, now entering its twentieth year. The Yup'iks continue to celebrate the annual return of the birds.

Another milestone was reached in 1999. Just before the turning of the new century, the United States and Canada formally amended the 1916 bird treaty. The amendments finally recognized traditional bird hunts in the North, thirty-eight years after the Barrow Duck-In. When bureaucrats implement this protocol amendment, the Inupiat Eskimos will no longer be criminals in their own land. I've heard that the implementation plan schedules the first legal spring season for 2003, the year of this chapter. Given history, I'll resist betting money just yet.

Caught within intractable political stalemates, negotiators sometimes pray for icebreakers. In the grips of tense and dangerous standoffs, the potential long-term fruits of small, humanizing acts, offered in good will, should never be discounted. Even the smallest of acts may help to ease the grip of cold mistrust, to break things loose.

At the end of the long, difficult negotiations at Chevak, we stood along the frozen dirt airstrip on the outskirts of town, awaiting the arrival of a bush plane to return us home. Several of us waited there, including delegates from California and Anchorage. An icy wind whistled. We stamped feet to stay warm. Unexpectedly, a solitary man on a three-wheeler came toward us from the distance, driving alone across the dry grassy space between the airstrip and town. He held a large sack between his legs. He stopped by us and killed the engine, a small weatherworn Yup'ik in dungarees, shorter than even me. I don't know who he was. He did not speak English, apparently. But he came up to each of us one by one to shake our hands. Then with a shy smile, he gave to each departing guest a small brown paper bag, taken from the sack on his seat. Our plane landed as he drove away. On the plane, we peered inside the bags. Each sack cradled tiny, freshly caught blackfish. Special farewell gifts to honor us.

Bibliographic Essay

Chapter One. Passing between Worlds

Kevin Starr writes about Henry J. Kaiser and housing in *Embattled Dreams: California in War and Peace, 1940–1950* (Oxford, UK: Oxford University Press, 2002, pp. 205–7). A general reference on the German Baptist Brethren, or Dunkers, known after 1908 as the Church of the Brethren, is *Brethren Society: The Cultural Transformation of a "Peculiar People,"* by Carl F. Bowman (Baltimore: John Hopkins University Press, 1995). The parable of building on rock and sand is found in the New Testament's book of Matthew (Matt. 7:24–27). Alaska's two subsistence laws are *Alaska Statutes* 16.05.258 (the state law) and the *Alaska National Interest Lands Conservation Act*, section 803, 16 U.S.C.A. 3113 (the federal law). The Behrends slide path on Mount Juneau is shown in *Avalanche!* (originally broadcast November 25, 1997, by NOVA, WGBA, Boston, Public Broadcasting System). Information from the U.S. Fish and Wildlife Service on the El Segundo Blue butterfly (*Euphilotes battoides allyni*), listed as endangered in 1976, can be found at Environmental Conservation Online System at http://ecos.fws.gov/. Dune & Prairie is the nonprofit organization coordinating volunteers to restore the dunes by the Los Angeles International Airport (http://dune-prairie.org). The rebirth of dancing on Nunivak Island is reported by Ted Horner in "From the Brink of Oblivion, Nunivak Islanders Revive the Spirit of Cup'iq Dance," *Delta Discovery*, December 18, 2002. *Pamyua* means "encore" or "once again," literally the "tail end of a dog," or by extension, the chorus of a song.

Chapter Two. Humanity

Mary Ciuniq Pete of Bethel helped with the word for the hairy being, *aarayulit*, which she indicates can be translated as "those who scream, moan, or holler." Its root, *aar-*, means "to say 'ah,' to open one's mouth and emit sound," according to the *Yup'ik Eskimo Dictionary*, by Steven A. Jacobson (Fairbanks: Alaska Native Language Center, University of Alaska, 1984). Ms. Pete reports that *miluquyulit* are another type of hairy being that throw things at you, a word now commonly applied to monkeys but also used to scare children from going off in the wilderness by themselves without an adult. The information on the ancient Indo-European root, *ghwer-*, derives from Appendix I: Indo-European Roots, in *The American Heritage Dictionary of the English Language*, 4th ed. (New York: Houghton Mifflin Company, 2000, p. 2030). James A. Fall of Anchorage helped me regarding the locations of feral cattle on the Aleutian Islands. Among the large literature on feral children are works by Charles Maclean, *The Wolf Children* (New York: Hill and Wang, 1977) and Lucien Malson, *Wolf Children and the Problem of Human Nature with the Wild Boy of Aveyron by Jean Itard* (New York: Monthly Review Press, 1972). Population densities are presented in the *U.S. Census 2000 Summary File 1 (SF1)*, GCT-PH1-R: Population, and GCT-PHT 1: Population, Housing Units, Area, and Density (http://factfinder.census.gov/).

Chapter Three. Respect

A Tlingit telling of "The Woman Who Married the Bear" is provided in *Haa Shuka, Our Ancestors: Tlingit Oral Narratives*, vol. 1, edited by Nora Marks Dauenhauer and Richard Dauenhauer (Seattle: University of Washington Press, 1987). In 2004 the Sealaska Heritage Institute (a Tlingit-Haida-Tsimshian nonprofit organization in southeast Alaska) and Juneau's Perseverance Theatre adapted "The Woman Who Married the Bear" for its summer children's theater arts program. They commissioned local playwright Merry Ellefson, who reviewed seventeen versions from the Tlingit, Athabascans, and

Tagish to create the final production version (*Juneau Empire*, August 6, 2004, www.sealaskaheritage.org/news/index.html). Robert Service's poem, "The Cremation of Sam McGee" can be found at www.geocities.com/Heartland/ Bluffs/8336/robertservice/sam.html. The epidemiological study on bears is "Human Injury from Bear Attacks in Alaska, 1900–1985" by John P. Middaugh (*Alaska Medicine* 29 [4]: 121–26). Currently, there are about sixteen thousand to twenty-four thousand black bears in California, according to the California Department of Fish and Game, *Living with California Black Bears*, February 2002. Ed Schoenfeld was the lyricist of the garbage bear song sung at the Juneau Folk Festival in 2001, and the music of "Ghost Riders in the Sky" was written by Stan Jones in 1949. According to Peter Blood and Annie Patterson (eds.) in *Rise Up Singing: The Group-Singing Song Book* (Bethlehem, Pa.: A Sing Out Publication, 1992: 76), a song about waltzing with bears originally appeared as "My Uncle Walter Waltzes with Bears" in *The Cat in the Hat Song Book* (© Dr. Seuss and Eugene Poddany, New York: Random House, 1967) with an adapted song, "Waltzing with Bears," claimed as an original composition (© Dale Marxen, Madison, Wis.: Tomorrow Music, 1986). In 2004, a picture of Taku, the glacier bear, was posted at www.alaskazoo.org/black_bear.htm. Mary Ciuniq Pete of Bethel provided helpful clarifications about Yup'ik beliefs regarding bears. In another helpful review, Susan Georgette of Kotzebue, Alaska, correctly remarked that the essay doesn't capture the "elemental fear" that can arise when living with small children in a remote log cabin with powerful brown bears nearby, knowing there's little a single human could do, short of self-defense with a weapon, to effectively resist any determined adult bear.

Chapter Four. Grace

The history of the butterfly effect, ascribed to Edward Lorenz, is provided by Michael Cross in *The Butterfly Effect* (www.cmp.caltech.edu/~mcc/chaos_new/Lorenz.html, February 27, 2001), who quotes from *Chaos and Nonlinear Dynamics*, by R. C. Hilborn (Oxford, UK: Oxford University Press, 1994). The finding of the middle of the world by Water Spider is told in "Zuni Origin Myths," compiled by Ruth L. Bunzel (*Forty-Seventh Annual Report of the Bureau of American Ethnology*, 1929–30 [Washington, D.C.: Smithsonian Institution, pp. 601–2]). Additional information on Black Mesa, the Navajo Generating Station, and Grand Canyon pollution is provided in *Cleaning Up the Navajo Generating Station* (Grand Canyon Trust, www.grandcanyontrust .org/programs/air/navajo.php); *Grand Canyon Air Pollution (Case No. 95, GRAND)* (Trade and Environmental Database, www.american.edu/TED/ SUPER.HTM); *Black Mesa, Arizona*, by Shannon Kelly (http://cpluhna.nau .edu/Places/black_mesa.htm); and "Native Americans and the Environment: A Survey of Twentieth Century Issues," by David R. Lewis (*American Indian Quarterly* 19 1995:423–50).

Chapter Five. Playing with Fish

The source for the history of sport fishing is *The Origins of Angling and a New Printing of "The Treatise of Fishing with an Angle,"* by John McDonald, assisted by Sherman Kuhn, Dwight Webster, and the editors of *Sports Illustrated* (Garden City, N.Y.: Doubleday and Company, 1963). Yup'ik word meanings provided in this chapter derive from the *Yup'ik Eskimo Dictionary*, by Steven A. Jacobson (Fairbanks: Alaska Native Language Center, University of Alaska, 1984). Basic ethnographic research in Togiak, Quinhagak, and Goodnews Bay was conducted in 1984 and reported in *Subsistence-Based Economies in Coastal Communities of Southwest Alaska*, by Robert J. Wolfe et al. (Technical Paper No. 89, Juneau: Division of Subsistence, Alaska Department of Fish and Game, 1984). Elizabeth Tukaya of Togiak served as the Yup'ik-English translator during interviews. As additional clarification, the Togiak, Kanektok, and Goodnews Rivers are three major salmon and char streams flowing into the Bering Sea. Five villages fish these rivers for food: Togiak and Twin Hills use the Togiak River; Goodnews Bay and Platinum use the Goodnews River; and Quinhagak uses the Kanektok River. At the time of this research, the villages also participated in small-scale commercial salmon fisheries near the mouths of each river, earning income for the relatively cash-poor area. In 1985 the five villages were predominantly Central Yup'ik Eskimo, with a combined population of 1,359 people. In 1987, 95 subsistence net sites were documented in the Togiak River, with the greatest concentration along the lower twelve miles (about 4.6 sites per river mile). In the early season (June through early August), elders accompanied by younger children often did the subsistence fishing, making day trips to set and tend nets for chinook, sockeye, and chum. Later (mid-August through mid-October), coho and char were harvested using small seines. Spawned sockeyes were harvested and dried by family groups at traditional fall camps at Togiak Lake, near the headwaters high in the mountains. The Togiak, Kanektok, and Goodnews Rivers were discovered in the 1970s by the Alaska sport guiding industry, consisting of guides and lodges offering recreational trips for sport fishing. In 1987 there were six lodges that transported fishers to the Togiak River. In a typical outing, sport anglers were flown by float-plane to temporary tent camps to fish from boats, sandbars, or the banks. Business owners were from outside the region, and 80 percent of the clientele were from outside the state. In 1986 there were 2,544 recreational visitors and 11,439 recreational use days on the Togiak, Kanektok, and Goodnews Rivers, based on lodge reports to Togiak National Wildlife Refuge. That is to say there were twice as many visitors as Yup'ik residents.

Chapter Seven. Profiting

This chapter presents a compilation of articles, editorials, and letters to the editor on the homeport topic that were originally printed by the primary newspaper for Alaska's capital city, the *Juneau Empire*, which graciously authorized their use. Materials are presented as they were originally published, including headlines, dates of release, and authors, except for a few shortened by me to reduce redundancy or to remove unrelated information. Three letters were not presented for the sake of space: a September 8, 1988, letter by George W. Davidson, an assemblyman who disagreed with the timing of the homeport vote; a September 28, 1988, letter by Bruce Weyhrauch, who cautioned that a yes vote might be misinterpreted to mean support for a homeport; and a September 29, 1988, letter by Mike McKee, who reiterated homeport issues covered by previous writers. All other letters on the homeport issue are presented in the chapter to the best of my knowledge. Larri Spengler and Steven Behnke of Juneau provided a helpful review of the chapter for the accuracy of historical events as they remembered them.

Chapter Eight. Icebreakers

The account of Jonah and the people of Nineveh is found in the prophets' book of Jonah in the Old Testament. Tom Rothe, of the Alaska Department of Fish and Game in Anchorage, helped me with information on recent bird trends in California and Alaska. A short history of migratory bird regulations pertaining to subsistence hunting in Alaska is provided in "Migratory Bird Subsistence Harvest in Alaska: Subsistence Harvest Regulations for Migratory Birds in Alaska during the Spring/Summer 2004 Subsistence Season, U.S. Fish and Wildlife Service, Final Rule" (50 CFR Part 92, RIN 1018-AJ27, *Federal Register* 69 [64]: 17318–29, April 2, 2004). The first international bird treaty was the Convention for the Protection of Migratory Birds in Canada and the United States, 1916, with ancillary treaties with Mexico (1936), Japan (1972), and Russia (1976). The lawsuit against the Yup'ik bird hunters was titled *The Alaska Fish and Wildlife Federation and Outdoor Council, Inc. and the Alaska Fish and Wildlife Fund, Inc., Plaintiffs-Appellants, v. Frank L. Dunkle, Director, United States Fish and Wildlife Service, and Donald Collinsworth, Commissioner of the Alaska Department of Fish and Game, Defendents-Appellees, with The Alaska Federation of Natives, The Association of Village Council Presidents, and Tony Vaska, Intervenors-Appellees.* The United States Court of Appeals for the Ninth Circuit ruled on the case in No. 86-3657, D.C. No. CV-84-013-V Opinion, October 9, 1987.

About the Author

Trained in cultural anthropology at UCLA, Robert J. Wolfe directed research on hunting and fishing by Alaska Natives and rural Alaska communities from 1982 to 2001 within the Alaska Department of Fish and Game. From 1977 to 1981 he taught at the University of Southern California. Currently, he works as a self-employed anthropologist from his home in North San Diego County. His publications on subsistence patterns of the Far North are applied works directed toward resolving conflicts faced by rural villages. This is his first collection of personal essays.